Anonymus

A letter to his excellency

The apostolic delegate in the East Indies

Anonymus

A letter to his excellency
The apostolic delegate in the East Indies

ISBN/EAN: 9783741172397

Manufactured in Europe, USA, Canada, Australia, Japa

Cover: Foto ©Andreas Hilbeck / pixelio.de

Manufactured and distributed by brebook publishing software
(www.brebook.com)

Anonymus

A letter to his excellency

PREFACE.

It has been thought useful to reprint the following Letter or Memorial, as but few Catholics, either in India or Europe, are in any way acquainted with the disastrous effects of the Portuguese Royal Patronage in India. Few Catholics know the way in which the manifest desires of successive Popes and the unanimous representations of the Missionary Bishops of India have been thwarted and nullified by the Portuguese Government and by a Goanese faction.

An appendix of documents referred to has been added to the original Letter.

Those unacquainted with these facts might think the language of this Letter, in parts, somewhat bold and uncompromising. It represents, however, the sentiments of the British Catholics of Bombay and Madras. Special care has been taken to verify all the facts.

It has been a painful task enough for Catholics to write in such terms about a Government which professes to be Catholic. To give, however, the full truth about the mischievous interference of Portugal in the religious affairs of India would justify the use of language far stronger than that contained in this Memorial.

Catholics are reminded that the Concordat of 1886 is not an ' ex cathedrâ ' pronouncement of the Holy See, any more than the Concordat of 1857, which was never carried out. Readers should also remember that this Letter to H. E. the Apostolic Delegate was of a semi-private nature, and that it has only been printed for private circulation among Catholics.

The British Catholics who form the Catholic Unions of Bombay and Madras yield to none in loyalty to their Queen, and fidelity to the Supreme Pontiff of the Church. They would be false to their country if they did not protest against the interference of a foreign Government in their Ecclesiastical concerns. They would be false to their religion if they did not inform the Holy Father's representative in the East Indies of the true state of the Church in British India.

The Joint Hon. Secretaries,
Bombay Catholic Union.

INDEX TO THE APPENDICES.

OFFICE OF THE BOMBAY CATHOLIC UNION,

MEDOWS STREET,

Bombay,   *July,* 1890.

To

H. E. MONSIGNOR A. AJUTI,

APOSTOLIC DELEGATE IN THE EAST INDIES,

OOTACAMUND.

YOUR EXCELLENCY,

As Joint Secretaries of the Bombay Catholic Union, we have been Part I. Paras 1.
to 18.
instructed by the Council of that Association, to express to Your Excellency the
feelings of surprise and sorrow caused to the Catholic subjects of Her Majesty
the Queen-Empress of India, in the Archdiocese of Bombay, by the recent
publication of the new Decree, signed at Rome on 5th March of this year,
regarding the further extension of extraordinary ecclesiastical jurisdiction granted
to the Portuguese Bishop of Damaun, the Most Rev. Dr. Da Costa, within the
limits of the Archdiocese of Bombay.

2. We are also desired to ask Your Excellency graciously to inform our
Holy Father Pope Leo XIII. of the loyal sentiments of his faithful children
the British Catholics, both European and Native-born, of the whole Province
of Bombay.

3. The views of the British Catholics of the Bombay Presidency regarding the continued exercise of ecclesiastical Patronage (or 'Padroado') by the
Crown of Portugal within the territory of the British Government in India, and
regarding the abnormal privileges enjoyed by Goanese immigrants, have been
already set forth in the humble Petition to the Holy Father which the Bombay
Catholic Union had lately the honour to forward through Your Excellency.
At the same time they forwarded a copy of their Memorial on this subject
addressed to the Marquis of Salisbury, Her Majesty's Minister for Foreign
Affairs.

4. The Catholic Union would have been content to await the development
of events, had not in the meantime the publication of the new Decree, now in
question, shown clearly that the Portuguese Government were more than ever
determined to push the pretensions of their ecclesiastical nominees in British

territory with an utter disregard of the ordinary laws and canons of the Church, and of the interests of religious peace and progress in India. Seizing apparently the opportunity of the vacancy caused in the See of Bombay by the death of the Most Rev. Archbishop Porter, the Portuguese Government have succeeded in undoing the work which that eminent and revered Prelate had effected, when he sought to find a working arrangement for the double jurisdiction in the Archdiocese of Bombay and the diocese of Damaun.

5. The Decrees passed by the Sacred Congregations of the Propaganda and of Extraordinary Ecclesiastical Affairs, in September and October 1887, have now been reversed by the new Decree, which grants such extraordinary indulgences and exceptional privileges to the Bishop of Damaun and to the subjects of the Padroado. Under the former Decrees the exemption of 'Padroadist' Catholics from the ordinary jurisdiction in Bombay was territorial. Under the present Decree that exemption becomes personal, and is extended by clause I. " to all those subjects of the Patronage, of Goan or Portuguese origin, who come from whatever part of India into the Bombay territory, in order to reside there."

6. By this provision, and by the other great concessions to the Bishops of the Patronage in the new Decree, the system of ' double jurisdiction' (declared by the Holy Father himself to be contrary to the canons of the Church and to the interests of religion) (cf. the Brief ' Studio et vigilantia,' of 26th August 1884) has received such an extension that, even were there no elements of discord existing already in the Archdiocese of Bombay, it would be exceedingly difficult to carry out the new provisions without friction and danger to the well-being of the Church.

7. The Bombay Catholic Union fully appreciate the objects of His Holiness the Pope in granting these extraordinary indulgences to the Bishop of Damaun, and in yielding once more to the persistent solicitations of the Ambassador Extraordinary of His Majesty the King of Portugal to the Holy See. His Holiness, in giving such a signal proof of favour to the Portuguese nation, fully believed that these concessions would be received in the same spirit in which they have been given, that the pretensions of the Crown of Portugal would at last be satisfied (cf. the last paragraph of clause I. of the new Decree,) and that lasting peace and concord would be established for the Catholic Church in India.

8. Were there any prospect whatever that these objects and wishes of our Holy Father the Pope would be fulfilled, then the British Catholics of India would loyally have submitted to all the concessions which the Holy See

has been pleased to make to the Portuguese claim of ' Patronage ' within British territory in India.

The Council of the Bombay Catholic Union, however, 'would be false to the duty they owe to the Holy Father and to Your Excellency, his Apostolic Delegate in the East Indies, if they did not disclose the fact that the new concessions have, in the same way as the former Decrees on the subject, been received by the Goanese and Portuguese Catholics of Bombay in such a spirit as leaves no hope that any concessions, however extreme, will ever lead to the results wished for by the Holy Father.

9. The leading organ of the so-called ' Padroadist' party in India is the newspaper styled the *Anglo-Lusitano*. This is the very print which was severely censured two years ago, in a letter from H. E. Cardinal Rampolla himself, for its violent and schismatical language. This censure was never published in his diocese by the Bishop of Damaun for the peculiar reason, apparently, that it had not received the Royal ' Placet' of Portugal. Moreover the Bishop of Damaun has continued to patronize this journal. He has even made it an official channel, at present, for publishing the new Decree. It may here be noted that the Decrees of 1887, referred to above, have never to this day been published in the diocese of Damaun. This is a course of conduct which has been a source of no little scandal in this Presidency.

10. As for the present Decree, which is so favourable to the Portuguese party, it has been at once published in the *Anglo-Lusitano*, with certain comments by the editor, in his edition of 1st May, 1890. A few examples will be given to show the spirit in which the newspaper, which the Bishop of Damaun delights to honour, speaks of the gracious concessions of the Holy See:— (A copy of this paper has been sent separately to Your Excellency.)

(a). In these comments not one word of thanks or gratitude is expressed to the Holy See. On the contrary, the insulting phrase is used that, in making these concessions, " the Propaganda have thrown a sop to Cerberus." The " Propaganda " is the term applied by the Portuguese or 'Padroadist' party in India to our Holy Father the Pope, and the Sacred Congregation of Cardinals. " Cerberus," it appears, is the term given to the " Padroado " by its own supporters.

(b). Complaint is made that the concessions were not extended at least to the city of Poona. It is remarked that " the Padroadists of Poona, Calcutta, and Madras have been entirely ignored," and the condescension of the Holy Father is stigmatised as 'an adroit move,'.

intended to conciliate " the Portuguese community of Bombay, the most powerful body of Padroadists in India, so that the less powerful may be left to themselves."

(c). Thinly-veiled threats are used to show that the last Decree will only be used by the Padroadist party as an additional reason for pressing for further and greater concessions from the Holy See. Allusion is made by the Goanese writer to the desire of His Holiness (expressed in clause I of the Decree) for an arrangement with the Portuguese Government 'more in conformity with the rules of the sacred canons,' and the opportunity is taken of complaining that the Archdiocese of Bombay was ever established by the Holy See at the creation of the Indian Hierarchy in 1886.

(Modo Sacro-
rum Canonum
dispositionibus
conformiori.)

(d). Clause I of the Decree also directs that a catalogue is to be made out of all the persons in Bombay who were subject to the Patronage at the date of the Concordat of 1886. The *Anglo-Lusitano* turns this provision into ridicule, and tries to evade it by the quibble that the Archdiocese of Bombay did not come into existence till about two months after the Concordat.

(e). This newspaper also remarks that " several other points that had been raised in connection with the Vatican Decrees, such as the residence of the Bishop of Damaun, have apparently been left undecided, unless indeed previous decisions are to hold good." This is disingenuous in the extreme when the writer had before him the letter of Your Excellency, (dated 19th April, 1890, and published in the *Bombay Catholic Examiner* of the 25th April) which states, in the very plainest language, that it is the wish of His Holiness that the regulations laid down in the former Decrees, except in so far as they have now been modified, should be carried into effect without delay."

11. Other sentiments, disloyal to Catholic principles, are uttered both in the English and Portuguese portions of the *Anglo-Lusitano*, but enough has been quoted to show in what spirit the extraordinary indulgences of the Holy See have been received.

In fact, the past and present attitude of the Padroadist party towards the Holy See and towards the Missionaries sent out by it to save the Catholic Church in India from ruin, give every reason to fear that if the new Decree is carried at once into execution, the Portuguese agitators in India and Europe will make every effort to obtain fresh concessions for the 'Padroado' and to undo the work of peace and progress initiated by the happy establishment of the Hierarchy in India, by the Holy Father. There can, unfortunately, be little doubt that these same agitators will, as in the past, stir up the passions of the ignorant multitude of Goanese immigrants in British India. They will point to the concessions already obtained as having been the fruit of their own efforts and a 'premium' (so to speak) on further agitation and insubordination.

12. Under the new Decree the question of the "double jurisdiction" would enter upon a new phase, which would afford peculiar opportunities for friction and difficulties of all kinds. There is no reason to hope that the Padroadist party in India has changed its old nature. It is needless to remind Your Excellency of the days when, after the issue of the Apostolic Brief ' Multa praeclare' in 1838, this party, in the devotion it professed to the Portuguese Crown, preferred disloyalty to the Church, and even schism, to obeying the lawful commands of the Sovereign Pontiff. The conduct of the Goanese agitators during and after the negociations which led to the Concordat of 1886, not to speak of the present schism in Ceylon, prove only too well that the old spirit of disloyalty and disobedience has not been cast out.

13. It may perhaps be said that the sentiments alluded to are held only by an extreme party of Goanese in India, and that they may not be shared by the Portuguese Government. The whole history, however, of the ' Portuguese Padroado' in India is quite against this supposition. The dissensions which led to the Concordat of 1857, and the negociations connected with the Concordat of 1886 clearly prove the closest connection between the Padroadist party in India and the Portuguese Government in Europe. The very Decree now in question is a further proof of this. The exemption of all Goanese in Bombay from the ecclesiastical jurisdiction of the Ordinary is, truly speaking, a matter of interest only to the Padroadist party in Bombay itself. Yet we find that the Portuguese Government instructed its Envoy at the Vatican to obtain this concession from the Holy See by pressing solicitations.

14. Taking all the above circumstances into consideration, the Council of the Bombay Catholic Union feel themselves bound to urge Your Excellency, most earnestly and respectfully, to exercise that Apostolic authority with which You have been graciously invested by our Holy Father Pope Leo XIII, for the welfare and concord of the Church in the East Indies.

The Catholic Union fully understand that Your Excellency, in Your capacity of Delegate Apostolic in India and Representative of the Holy Father, is not empowered to vary in any way the provisions of the Concordat of 1886 or the explanatory Decrees which the ecclesiastical authorities at Rome may be pleased to pass in virtue thereof. Nor do the Bombay Catholic Union ask Your Excellency to take any action against the said Concordat of 1886.

15. By the wisdom and forethought of our Holy Father, the appointment of Your Excellency as Apostolic Delegate in the East Indies enables you, by your presence on the spot, to judge accurately what are the special dangers which assail the Church in India. Your Excellency, therefore, is especially fitted to act as the official intermediary between the Holy Father and his faithful children, the British Catholics of India.

16. Upon all these considerations the Bombay Catholic Union humbly beg Your Excellency to consider whether the true interests of the Church in India will not best be served by taking what immediate steps may seem best for postponing the further execution of the last Decree, until the arrival of the Archbishop who is still to be appointed to the See of Bombay. Should Your Excellency consider that your position does not allow you to take any immediate action in the mater, we pray you to make a reference to Rome on the subject.

17. The members of the Union feel confident that Your Excellency fully appreciates the grave dangers and inconveniences which will ensue from carrying out the far-reaching changes contained in the new Decree, in the absence of the recognised head of the Archdiocese of Bombay. In this Archdiocese at the present time we see, on the one side, a party animated with the sentiments which have always guided the Goanese 'Padroadists' of India, and on the other side, the British Catholics of the regular jurisdiction, standing (so to speak) "as sheep without a shepherd," that is, without an Archbishop who could effectually represent and defend the interests of his flock and of the Church.

18. It is also our duty respectfully to point out that all concessions made to the Portuguese Government, of the kind embodied in the last Decree, will make an equitable settlement of the question of ' double jurisdiction ' all the more difficult when that question comes to be settled in a rational manner. All British Catholics in India look forward to the day when the Government of Her Majesty the Queen-Empress will be ready to negociate with the Holy See regarding the position of the Church in India, and to co-operate with the Holy Father in securing religious peace in India on a firm and stable basis. The mission of General Sir Lintorn Simmons to Rome led British Catholics to think and to hope that, that day is close at hand. Though disappointed in their hopes in that mission, their expectations have been once more raised by the appointment

of Sir Adrian Dingli as Envoy Extraordinary of Her Majesty the Queen-Empress
to the Vatican. They look forward hopefully to the day when the anachronism
of the Portuguese Patronage will cease to exist in Bombay and other parts of
British India. They are convinced that this will be the only satisfactory
solution of the vexed question of the 'double jurisdiction.'

(*Part II. Disastrous effects of the 'Padroado' in India, and conclusion—
paras. 19 to 32.*)

19. In making these representations we do not lose sight of the well-known
fact that the Holy See has, by its Papal Briefs and Bulls, shown the utmost
solicitude for the peace and progress of the Church in India, and that in tolerat-
ing the Portuguese " Padroado " in this country and in making so many concessions to the Goanese agitators, it has often had (if we may so express it) to sacrifice India for the sake of religious peace in Portugal. We hope, however, that
we in India may be excused if, looking at the case from the local point of view,
we represent to Your Excellency the disastrous effects which these repeated
concessions and continual changes in policy produce *in India itself.* Such changes
and concessions have been and are, unfortunately, destructive of the authority of
the Holy See and of all real respect and obedience to the same. The authority of
the Holy See cannot be weakened without equal injury to the authority of the
Bishops and Missionaries. It is hardly necessary to point out to Your Excellency
that the State of the Church in India and the temperament of the majority of Indian Catholics are such, that it is disastrous thus to weaken the bonds of discipline.

20. Even to well-instructed European Catholics, these continual concessions
and changes are bewildering, but such persons can more or less appreciate the
difficulties which encompass the Holy Father, and understand that in giving
his sanction to measures which, in the opinion of Bishops and Missionaries,
are an unmixed evil for the Church in India, and offensive to the vast majority
of British Catholics, he is necessarily actuated by other than merely local
considerations.

21. With the bulk of Indian Catholics, however, the case is otherwise.
Many of the Native Christians, especially in the South of India, are simple
cultivators and fishermen. Simple people, such as these, cannot be expected to
appreciate the peculiar difficulties of the Holy See in Europe. They judge only
from what they see. They know nothing of the difficulties of the Church in
Portugal. They know nothing of the demands of European policy. They
know nothing of the " Roman Question. " They have been taught to respect
and obey the Holy Father, and nearly all of them are well disposed to render
a hearty obedience to him as supreme in religious affairs. They have, however,
seen successive Popes in the most definite and apparently irrevocable manner

practically abolish the "Padroado," and condemn and even excommunicate rebellious Goanese priests, and then without a word of explanation the Papal documents are allowed by Rome to become a dead letter, simply because Portugal opposes them. The result is that Catholics in India are unable to attach any importance to Roman documents condemning the abuses of the Portuguese Patronage. Bad Catholics know that they have only to fight against them, or ignore them for a sufficiently long time, and they will get what they want. Good Catholics have to stand by bewildered and discouraged. They are forced to wonder why the Pope yields so much of his authority over the Church in India to the King of Portugal.

22.   We respectfully beg Your Excellency to consider how many times, during the last fifty years, have Briefs and Decrees been published in India all equally emphatic, and all equally definitive in language, only to become a dead letter, or to be soon followed by others contradicting or undoing the provisions of the preceding ones.   How often have Indian Catholics seen the unanimous representations of their Bishops and their own Memorials, apparently ignored, while the utmost deference has been paid to the wishes of a weak but meddlesome foreign Government, and to the clamour of a noisy and worthless faction.

° (E. G. the Memorials of the Kárwár Catholics, and of the Bombay East Indian Association)

23.   We will not weary Your Excellency with numerous examples to illustrate these remarks.   The history of the Church in India during the last fifty years is only too full of instances which show the disastrous effects of concessions in favour of the "Padroado."   What could have been more emphatic than the Brief "Multa praeclare" (28th April 1838) which abolished the four Portuguese bishoprics of Cochin, Cranganore, Mylapor and Malacca and limited the jurisdiction of the Archbishop of Goa to the Portuguese possessions : or the Brief "Probe nostis" (9th May 1853), which condemned the Indo-Portuguese schism, and excommunicated four rebellious priests ?   And they ended in the abortive Concordat of 1857.   The Brief "Studio et vigilantia" (26th August 1884) was emphatic and final.   In it the Holy Father stated that the state of the Church in India was unsatisfactory, that grave disturbances had taken place, that there was reason to fear that the faith of Catholics would be imperilled, the conversion of infidels impeded and the growth of religion thwarted.   The Holy Father traced these evils to the "double jurisdiction," and he accordingly *abolished the same in seven Vicariates.*   What was the result ?   The Brief remained a dead letter, and to the discouragement of good Catholics and to the triumph of the "Padroadist" faction, it was followed by the Concordat of 1886, in which the "double jurisdiction" was, as it were, sanctified and perpetuated.

24. In Madras a Catholic Union has lately been formed on much the same lines as the Bombay Catholic Union, with the full sanction and approval of no less than thirteen Archbishops and Bishops of Southern India. It will be the duty of the Council of that Union, at a convenient opportunity, to lay before Your Excellency the disastrous effects which the Concordat of 1886 and the pressure of Portugal upon the Holy See have had on the peace and prosperity of the Church in that Province. We have, however, been urged now to inform Your Excellency, that the British Catholics of Madras, and all the Catholics of that Archdiocese, have been deeply pained by the way in which their distinguished Archbishop, Dr. Colgan, has been humiliated in the sight of the whole population, by the provisions of the Concordat of 1886 in favour of a foreign Government like that of Portugal. What they have felt especially is the fact that even the Concordat of 1886 was not allowed by Portugal to be duly carried out in Madras.

25. On 19th January, 1887, Monsignor Agliardi, Your Excellency's august predecessor actually executed this Concordat in the town of Madras, and those Catholics who were formerly of the Goanese jurisdiction accepted, quite contentedly, the rule of Archbishop Colgan. Two months later the work was undone by an order from Rome, and in deference to Portugal the "double jurisdiction" was restored. This retrograde measure was all the more astounding to the clergy and laity of the Archdiocese of Madras, as their Archbishop had already, under the terms of the Concordat, had to sacrifice a large portion of his continuous territory to the revived Portuguese Diocese of Mylapore. Again, the schismatics of Kottayam, Trichur and the Malabar Coast cannot understand the alterations which the Holy See makes in decisions which it has declared to be definitive. They look on these constant changes as new proofs against the wisdom and the infallibility of the Holy See. This is a fresh obstacle to conversions. The Bishops lose the confidence of the people, since Rome, the fountain-head of authority, seems to contradict herself.

26. This is not the place nor is it our duty, to lay before Your Excellency at any greater length the special griefs of the Catholics of Madras. We will only point out that in Madras as in Bombay, the wishes and interests of British Catholics are entirely ignored. No attention has been paid to the representations of Archbishop Colgan, the only British prelate now (save one) in India, while concessions are lavished upon the subjects of the Portuguese Patronage and on the followers of the "*Anglo-Lusitano.*" Another British prelate, Archbishop Porter, (unhappily now no more) was listened to for a while in Rome,

and was able to introduce some order into the chaos of the "double jurisdiction" in Bombay. Now that he is dead and has sacrificed his life in the service of God's Church, his work is undone by what must have been extreme pressure on the part of the Portuguese Ambassador in Rome. In the insulting words of the triumphant *Anglo-Lusitano*,— "the Propaganda have thrown a sop to Cerberus!"

27. We have already written at length concerning this Goanese paper. We will only now remind Your Excellency of the way in which the *Anglo-Lusitano* treated the Decree of 17th September, 1887, declared by the subsequent Decree of 25th September, 1888, to be "absolute and definitive." These Decrees regarding the regulation of the double jurisdiction were not only treated with abuse and contumely by the *Anglo-Lusitano*, but were also utterly ignored by the Portuguese Bishops of Damaun and Mylapore. These Bishops have never even published the Papal Decree of 1888 in their dioceses. The language of the *Anglo-Lusitano* was, however, too violent to pass unnoticed in Rome. In his famous letter of 21st December, 1888, condemning this news-paper, the Cardinal Secretary of State stigmatised the resistance of the Goanese to these Decrees as 'insane.' But what happened next? The *Anglo-Lusitano* made no submission, and the Bishop of Damaun, as already stated, has actually refused to publish the censure of the Cardinal Secretary of State. All faithful Catholics have waited for the Holy See to vindicate its outraged authority, and to support its missionary priests and Bishops, who had been so grossly insulted by the Portuguese faction. Moreover, we have been informed that, on 9th January, 1889, the missionary Archbishops and Bishops of India, headed by the late Archbishop Porter, sent a Memorial to the Holy See praying it not to modify its Decree or yield to the Goanese agitation which it had already condemned. The Holy See has done nothing of the kind. On the contrary all the concessions for which the *Anglo-Lusitano* clamoured have been granted. The triumph of the Padroadist agitators is complete, *i. e.*, of those very people whom H. E. Cardinal Rampolla stigmatised 'as ignorant and corrupt.'

28. Enough has now been written to prove to Your Excellency that British Catholics have reason to say that the policy of the Holy See towards the 'Padroado' in India has had disastrous effects and that good Catholics are bewildered and discouraged by it. At the same time we sincerely trust that Your Excellency will not consider the frankness of these remarks disrespectful. We have written frankly on behalf of the British Catholics of Bombay and Madras, because we felt sure that Your Excellency would prefer to know the

real truth concerning the state of the Church in those parts ;from residents on the spot, and to learn the real sentiments of Catholics, both British and Native born, who are the subjects of the Paramount Power of India. We wish merely to present the case as it must appear to the majority of Indian Catholics. Moreover it is well known that, before the Concordat of 1886 the missionary Bishops of the South of India gave it as their unanimous opinion that, * (Memorial of the Bishops of the Madras presidency to the Secretary of State for India dated 15th August 1883.) in these days the " Padroado" is an unmixed evil, and that the best solution of the present difficulties lies in its abolition. They were strengthened in this opinion by the Brief ' Studic et vigilantia' of the year 1884, nor has the history of the. " Padroado " since the Concordat of 1886 given one any reason to hold that this opinion is incorrect.

29.   We have written to Your Excellency from a full heart, and with perfect confidence in Your justice and love of truth.   Our sole object in Bombay and Madras, is to let Your Excellency and the Holy See know the true feelings of the Catholics of British India, so that the proper remedies may be applied and peace and prosperity restored to the Church.   India is perhaps the finest field for successful missionary work in the whole world.   Owing, however, to the blighting influence of the Portuguese Patronage and the interference of the Portuguese Government, the beneficent work of the devoted missionaries of the Church is stunted and withered over vast portions of the Indian Peninsula.

30.   It has been a painful duty for us to describe, even in part, the disastrous effects of the Portuguese Royal Patronage in India.   Our task, however, will not have been in vain if we lead all reasonable men to the one, inevitable conclusion, that the sole remedy for all these ills is the total abolition of the "Padroado" in British India.   The indulgence and the condescension of the Holy Father have been too long abused by a self-seeking Government in Europe, and by interested agitators in India.   The day for concessions is passed.   *Salus animarum suprema lex.*   If ever the Catholic religion is to flourish in India the " Padroado' must be destroyed root and branch.   We do not hesitate to press the subject to this, its only logical conclusion.   We know, from historical facts and from weighty documents, that, as far back as the 17th century, successive Popes have found the institution of the Portuguese Patronage in the East a hindrance to religion instead of a help, a curse instead of a blessing.

31.   We trust that Your Excellency will kindly make our position clear to our Holy Father the Pope.   The " Bombay Catholic Union " is not composed merely of European Catholics.   By far the larger proportion of members are East Indians, or Native-born Catholics, who are British subjects.   Moreover the

parent association in Bombay has already two flourishing Branches, one in Poona and another in Karwar. The latter Branch is composed entirely of native-born Catholics. We are also entitled to speak on behalf of the "Bombay East Indian Association," which represents a large and rising community in Bombay and its neighbourhood. Its members are all British subjects and have full right to be heard, as they are the permanent native-born Catholics of those parts. They are loyal subjects of the British Government, and deeply resent the pretentious claims of the Portuguese Crown in British India. Lastly, we plead for justice on behalf of the thousands of Irish soldiers who are to be found in the British army in India, and who want no Portuguese "Patron" to come between them and our Holy Father the Pope.

32. In conclusion we respectfully beg Your Excellency kindly to inform our Holy Father Pope Leo XIII, of all our sentiments together with the assurance of our deepest love and veneration, so that His Holiness may be kept fully informed of the hopes and wishes of his faithful children, the Catholics of British India. In order that the ecclesiastical authorities at Rome may, as speedily as possible be informed of the state of affairs in India we have the honour to forward a French translation together with this letter to Your Excellency.

Trusting to receive a favourable answer, and assuring Your Excellency of the deepest respect and veneration of the whole Bombay Catholic Union.

We remain,

Your Excellency's

Most faithful and humble servants in Christ,

Joint Secretaries,
Bombay
Catholic Union.

3

BUREAU DE L UNION CATHOLIQUE DE BOMBAY
MEDOWS STREET,

BOMBAY,

Juillet, 1890.

A SON EXCELLENCE

MONSEIGNEUR A. AJUTI,

ARCHEVÊQUE D'ACRIDA, DÉLÉGUÉ APOSTOLIQUE AUX INDES ORIENTALES.

OOTACAMUND.

EXCELLENCE,

Comme Secrétaires associés de l'Union Catholique de Bombay, le Conseil de cette Union nous a chargé d'exprimer à Votre Excellence les sentiments de surprise et de douleur qu'a causé aux sujets catholiques de S. M. la Reine-Impératrice des Indes, dans l'archidiocèse de Bombay, la récente publication du nouveau décret signé à Rome le 5 mars de cette année, relativement à l'extension plus grande de la juridiction Ecclésiastique Extraordinaire accordée à Mgr. l'Evêque portugais de Damaum, le très Révérend Docteur Da Costa, dans les limites de l'archidiocèse de Bombay.

2. On nous chargé aussi de prier Votre Excellence de vouloir bien faire connaître à notre Saint Père le Pape, les sentiments de ses fidèles enfants les catholiques britanniques, soit européens soit indigènes, de toute la province de Bombay.

3. Les vues des catholiques anglais de la Présidence de Bombay touchant la continuation du droit de Patronage Ecclésiastique ou " l'adroado" exercé par la couronne de Portugal sur le territoire du gouvernement anglais dans l'Inde, et les privilèges inouis dont jouissent les immigrants goanais, ont déja été exposés dans une humble pétition au Saint Père, que l'Union Catholique de Bombay eut dernièrement l'honneur d'envoyer par l'entremise de Votre Excellence. En même temps elle adressait une copie de son Mémoire sur ce sujet, au Marquis de Salisbury, Ministre de Sa Majesté pour les Affaires Etrangères.

4. L'Union Catholique se serait contentée d'attendre les événements, si, dans l'intervalle, la publication du nouveau Décret en question, n'était venue

prouver clairement que le gouvernement portugais était plus que jamais déterminé à soutenir les prétentions de ses représentants ecclésiastiques dans l'Inde anglaise ; et cela, avec le plus profond mépris des lois ordinaires et des Canons de l'Eglise, ainsi que des intérêts de la paix et du progrès de la religion dans l'Inde. Profitant évidemment de la vacance produite sur le siège de Bombay, par la mort de l'Archévêque, le très Révérend Porter, le gouvernement portugais a réussi à défaire l'œuvre que cet éminent et vénéré prélat avait effectuée, en trouvant un "modus vivendi" tolérable pour la "double juridiction" dans l'archidiocèse de Bombay et le diocèse de Damaum.

5. Les Décrets publiés en réponse à des questions, par la Sacrée Congrégation de la Propagande et celle des Affaires Ecclésiastiques Extraordinaires en Septembre et en Octobre 1887, viennent d'être annullés par le nouveau Décret, qui accorde des faveurs si extraordinaires et des privilèges si exceptionnels à l'evêque de Damaum et aux sujets du Padroado. En vertu des premiers Décrets, l'exemption des catholiques "Padroadistes" de la juridiction ordinaire à Bombay était territoriale. Par la teneur du dernier Décret, cette exemption devient personnelle, et est étendue par l'article I. à tous les sujets du Patronage, d'origine goanaise ou portugaise qui viennent de quelque part de l'Inde que ce soit, dans le territoire de Bombay pour y résider."

6. Par cette décision et par les autres grandes concessions faites aux évêques du Padroado sous le nouveau Décret, le système de la "double juridiction" que le Saint Père lui-même a déclaré contraire aux Canons de l'Eglise et aux intérêts de la religion (cf. le Bref *Studio et Vigilantia*, du 26 Août 1884), a reçu une extension telle, que même supposant l'absence des éléments de discorde qui existent déjà dans l'Archidiocèse de Bombay, il serait extrêmement difficile de mettre à exécution ces nouvelles dispositions sans causer des froissements et sans péril pour le bien de l'Eglise.

7. L'Union Catholique de Bombay comprend parfaitement le but de notre Saint Père le Pape en accordant ces faveurs extraordinaires à l'évêque de Damaum et en cédant une fois de plus aux instantes sollicitations de l'Ambassadeur extraordinaire de Sa Majesté le Roi de Portugal, près du Saint Siège. Sa Sainteté en accordant une si grande marque de faveur à la nation portugaise était pleinement convaincue que ces concessions seraient reçues dans le même esprit avec lequel elles avaient été données. Elle pensait que les prétentions de la couronne de Portugal seraient enfin satisfaites (cf. le dernier paragraphe de l'article I. du nouveau Décret), et qu'une paix durable et une parfaite harmonie régneraient dans l'Eglise de l'Inde.

8. S'il y avait le moindre espoir fondé que ces vues et ces désirs de Sa Sainteté seront réalisés, les catholiques britanniques de l'Inde se soumettraient loyalement à toutes les concessions que le Saint Siège a daigné accorder aux prétentions du Padroado sur le territoire anglais.

Mais le Conseil de l'Union Catholique de Bombay manquerait gravement à son devoir envers Sa Sainteté et envers Votre Excellence, son Délégué Apostolique dans les Indes Orientales, s'il ne révélait ce fait, que comme les Décrets antérieurs sur la matière, les nouvelles concessions ont été reçues par les catholiques portugais et goanais de Bombay, avec un esprit qui ne laisse aucun espoir d'atteindre jamais par des concessions, quelles qu'elles soient, le but poursuivi par le Saint Père.

9. L'organe principal du soi-disant parti du Padroado, dans les Indes, est le journal qui s'intitule " *Anglo-Lusitano.*" C'est cette même feuille que Son Eminence le Cardinal Rampolla lui-même, il y a deux ans, blâma sévèrement dans une lettre, pour ses violences de langage et ses tendances schismatiques. Cette censure, l'évêque de Damaum ne l'a jamais publiée dans son diocèse, sans doute par la raison singulière que cette lettre n'avait pas reçu le " Placet royal " du Portugal. De plus l'évêque de Damaum n'a pas cessé de patronner ce journal ; il en a même fait son organe officiel, pour promulguer le nouveau Décret. D'autre part, on peut remarquer ici que les Décrets de 1887, mentionnés plus haut, n'ont pas encore été publiés dans le diocèse de Damaum. C'est là une conduite qui certainement semble exiger une justification devant Votre Excellence et auprès de Sa Sainteté.

10. Quant au Décret nouveau si favorable au parti portugais, il a été publié sans retard dans l'*Anglo-Lusitano*, avec les commentaires du rédacteur, dans le No. du 1er Mai 1890. Un petit nombre de citations feront connaître dans quel esprit ce journal que l'évêque de Damaum honore de son patronage parle des gracieuses concessions du Saint Siège. [On a envoyé séparément à votre Excellence un numero de ce journal.]

(a). Dans ces commentaires on ne lit pas un seul mot de remerciment ou de reconnaissance à l'égard du Saint Siège. On contraire on y trouve cette phrase insultante, qu'en faisant ces concessions "La Propagande a jeté un os a Cerbère pour l'apaiser."—" La Propagande " est le terme employé par les partisans du Padroado pour désigner Notre Saint Père le Pape, et les Sacrées Congrégations des Cardinaux. Cerbère, parait-il, est le nom donné au Padroado par ses propres partisans. [" Have thrown a sop to Cerberus " (d'après l'original).]

4

(*b*). On se plaint de ce que les concessions n'aient pas été étendues au moins jusqu'à la ville de Poona. On lit par exemple que les " Padroadistes de Poona, Calcutta et Madras ont été complétement negligés," et la condescendance du Saint Père est stigmatisée du nom de " manœuvre habile " qui avait pour objet de gagner " la communauté portugaise de Bombay, la plus puissante parmi les Padroadistes de l' Inde, pour abandonner les autres qui sont plus faibles, à elles-mêmes."

(*c*). D' un ton menaçant qui se dissimule à peine, on dit que le dernier Décret sera seulement une raison de plus pour les Padroadistes de persis- ter dans leurs réclamations, afin d'arracher de plus grandes concessions au Souverain Pontife. L' écrivain goanais fait une allusion au désir de Sa Sainteté (exprimé dans la première clause du Décret) d'un arrangement avec le gouvernement portugais "plus conforme aux dispositions des saints Canons ;" et il saisit cette occasion pour se plaindre de l'érection de l'Archidiocèse de Bombay par le Saint Siège, lors de l'établissement de la Hiérarchie dans l'Inde.

'Modo Sacro-
rum Canonum
dispositionibus
conformior.'

(*d*). La première clause du Décret ordonne de faire un Catalogue de toutes les personnes de Bombay qui etaient soumises au Padroado à la date du Concordat de 1886. L' *Anglo-Lusitano* tourne en ridicule cette disposition, et il s'efforce de l'esquiver par la mauvaise raison que l' Archidiocèse de Bombay n'a commencé à exister qu'environ deux mois après le Concordat.

(*e*). Ce même journal fait aussi remarquer que plusieurs autres questions qui " avaient été posées à l'occasion des Décrets du Vatican, comme par exemple, celle de la résidence de l' évêque de Damaum, ont été apparem- ment laissées sans réponse, à moins que les décisions antérieures ne doivent rester en vigueur." Or, c'est là une assertion absolument dénuée de sincérité. Le rédacteur avait devant lui la lettre de Votre Excellence (datée du 1 d'avril 1890 et publiée dans le " *Bombay Ca- tholic Examiner* " du 25 avril), où il est dit dans les termes les plus clairs, que la volonté de Sa Sainteté est que toutes les décisions arrêtées précédemment soient mises en exécution sans délai, sauf celles qui viennent d'être récemment modifiées.

11. D'autres sentiments contraires aux principes catholiques se trouvent exprimés dans les deux parties, anglaise et portugaise, de l' *Anglo-Lusitano*. Mais nous avons fourni assez de citations pour montrer dans quel esprit les conces- sions extraordinaires du Saint Siège ont été reçues.

De fait, l'attitude passée et présente du parti padroadiste à l'égard du Saint Siège et des missionaires envoyés par lui pour sauver de la ruine l'Eglise catholique dans l'Inde donne toute raison de craindre que, si le présent décret est exécuté sur le champ, les agitateurs portugais dans l'Inde et en Europe, ne fassent tous leurs efforts pour obtenir de nouvelles concessions en faveur du Padroado, et ruiner ainsi l'œuvre de paix et de progrès que le Saint Père a si heureusement commencée en établissant la Hiérarchie dans l'Inde. Il n'y a malheureusement pas lieu de douter que ces mêmes agitateurs ne continuent, comme par le passé, à exciter les passions de la multitude ignorante des immigrants goanais dans l'Inde britannique. Ils leur représenteront les concessions déjà obtenues comme le fruit de leurs constants efforts, et en quelque sorte comme une " prime d'encouragement " pour les engager à recourir encore à l'agitation et à la révolte.

12. Par suite du nouveau Décret la question de la double juridiction entrerait dans une phase nouvelle qui offrirait de nombreuses occasions de conflits et de difficultés de tout genre. Il n'y a pas lieu de croire que le parti padroadiste dans l'Inde ait changé de nature. Il est inutile de rappeler à Votre Excellence le temps qui suivit la publication du Bref apostolique "Multa præclare" en 1838, lorsque ce parti, dans son absolu dévouement aux intérêts portugais, préféra la révolte ouverte contre l'Eglise, même le schisme, plutôt que d'obéir aux ordres légitimes du Souverain Pontife. La conduite des agitateurs goanais pendant et après les négotiations qui amenèrent le Concordat de 1886, pour ne rien dire du présent schisme de Ceylon, ne prouvent que trop bien, qu'ils n'ont rien dépouillé de cet esprit de révolte et de désobeissance.

13. On pourrait peut être objecter que les sentiments auxquels nous faisons allusion sont tout au plus ceux d'un parti extrême de goanais dans l'Inde, et ne sont nullement partagés par le gouvernement portugais. Cependant toute l'histoire du Padroado portugais est contre une telle supposition. Les dissensions qui amenèrent le Concordat de 1857 et les négociations qui accompagnèrent celui de 1886 prouvent clairement qu'il y a une étroite connexion entre le parti Padroadiste dans l'Inde et le gouvernement portugais en Europe. Le dernier décret qui nous occupe en est une nouvelle preuve. A vrai dire, l'exemption de tous les goanais de Bombay de la juridiction de l'Ordinaire n'intéresse que les Padroadistes de Bombay. Toutefois nous voyons que le gouvernement portugais chargea son ambassadeur près du Vatican d'obtenir du Saint Siège cette concession par ses pressantes sollicitations.

14. Pour toutes ces considerations, le Conseil de l'Union Catholique de Bombay se croit obligé de prier très instamment et très respectueusement Votre

Excellence d'user de cette autorité Apostolique dont vous avez été révêtu par le Souverain Pontife Léon XIII, pour la prospérité et la concorde de l'Eglise aux Indes. L'Union Catholique comprend très bien que ces attributions de Légat Apostolique et de représentant du Saint Siège dans l'Inde, ne s'étendent pas jusqu' à vous permettre de changer en quoique ce soit les clauses du Concordat de 1886, ni les Décrets que les autorités ecclésiastiques à Rome jugent bon d'édicter pour en régler l'exécution. Aussi l'Union Catholique de Bombay ne demande-t-elle pas à Votre Excellence de porter aucune atteinte au Concordat de 1886.

15. Grâce à la sagesse et à la prévoyance du Saint Siège, la nomination de Votre Excellence comme Délégué Apostolique aux Indes Orientales, vous met à même, par votre présence sur les lieux, de juger en connaissance de cause des périls particuliers qui menacent l'Eglise dans l'Inde. Votre Excellence est donc dans les conditions les plus favorables pour servir d'intermédiaire officiel entre le Saint Siège et ses fidèles enfants, les catholiques de l'Inde britannique.

16. Pour tous ces motifs, l'Union Catholique de Bombay prie humblement Votre Excellence de voir si le bien de l'Eglise dans l'Inde n'exige pas que l'on prenne immédiatement les mesures qui sembleraient les plus opportunes, pour différer l'exécution entière du dernier Décret jusqu' à l'arrivée de l'Archevêque qui doit être désigné pour le siège de Bombay. Au cas si Votre Excellence jugerait que votre position ne vous permet pas de prendre une decision immédiate à ce sujet, nous vous prions d'en référer à Rome.

17. Les membres de l'Union Catholique ont la confiance que Votre Excellence se rend pleinement compte des graves dangers et des inconvénients qui suivront l'exécution des changements importants contenus dans le nouveau Décret, si elle a lieu en l'absence du chef reconnu de l'Archidiocèse de Bombay. Dans cet Archidiocèse nous voyons en ce moment, d'un côté, un parti animé des sentiments qui ont toujours guidé les partisans goanais du Padroado dans l'Inde, et de l'autre, les catholiques sujets britanniques de la juridiction régulière : ces derniers sont, pour ainsi dire, " comme des brebis sans pasteur,' c'est à dire, sans un Archevêque qui puisse effectivement représenter et défendre les intérêts de son troupeau et de l'Eglise.

18. C'est aussi notre devoir de faire remarquer respectueusement que toutes les concessions faites aux Portugais, dans le genre de celles contenues dans le dernier Décret, ne font que rendre plus difficile une solution équitable de la question de la double juridiction, le jour où on voudra la régler comme semble l'exiger la raison. Tous les catholiques anglais de l'Inde espèrent voir bientôt

7

le jour où le gouvernement de Sa Majesté la Reine-Impératrice sera prêt à négocier avec le Saint Siège sur l'état de l'Eglise aux Indes et à prêter son concours au Saint Père pour asseoir sur des bases solides et durables la paix religieuse dans ce pays. La mission à Rome de Sir Adrian Dingli, comme celle du Général Sir Lintorn Simmons, incline les catholiques sujets de Sa Majesté à croire que ce jour est tout près. Ce jour-là l'anachronisme du Patronage portugais cessera d'exister à Bombay et dans toute l'Inde-anglaise. Ce sera la seule solution satisfaisante de la question si débattue de la double juridiction.

IIème Partie. Paragraphe 19 jusqu'au para 32 (la fin).

19. En faisant ces représentations nous ne perdons pas de vue le fait notoire que le Saint Siège dans les Bulles et les Brefs Pontificaux a montré une extrême sollicitude pour la paix et le progrès de l'Eglise aux Indes, et qu' en tolérant le Padroado portugais dans ce pays, et en faisant tant de concessions à l'agitation goanaise, il a dû souvent, si on ose parler ainsi, sacrifier les Indes, pour obtenir la paix religieuse en Portugal. Nous espèrons cependant qu'on nous excusera, nous catholiques de l' Inde, d'envisager la situation à un point de vue local, et de représenter à Votre Excellence, les effets désastreux que ces concessions réitérées et ces fluctuations dans la politique produisent *dans l'Inde elle-même*. Ces changements et ces concessions ont été, et sont encore, malheureusement très préjudiciables à l'autorité du Saint Siège, au respect véritable, et à l'obéissance qui lui sont dûs. L'autorité du Saint Siège ne saurait être affaiblie sans que, par un contre-coup fatal, l'autorité des évêques et missionnaires ne souffre également. Il serait superflu de faire remarquer à Votre Excellence que, vu l'état de l'Eglise aux Indes, et la tournure d'esprit de la majorité des catholiques indiens, il serait désastreux d'affaiblir le nerf de la discipline.

20. Même pour des catholiques européens bien instruits, ces concessions et ces changements continuels sont de nature à les étonner, et cependant ils sont capables d'apprécier plus ou moins les difficultés qui entourent le Saint Père et comprendre qu'en sanctionnant des mesures qui, de l'avis des évêques et des missionnaires, sont désastreuses pour l'Eglise des Indes et injurieuses pour la grande majorité des sujets anglais catholiques, il est mû par d' autres motifs que des considérations d'interêt purement local.

21. Il en est tout autrement de la masse des catholiques indiens. La plupart des chrétiens indigènes, surtout dans le sud de l'Inde, sont de simples cultivateurs ou des pêcheurs. On ne saurait attendre d'une population aussi simple qu'elle puisse apprécier les difficultés spéciales du Saint Siège en Europe. Ils jugent seulement par ce qu'ils voient. Ils n'ont pas la moindre idée des

difficultés de l'Eglise en Portugal. Ils ne savent rien des exigences de la politique en Europe, rien de la Question Romaine. On leur a appris à respecter le Saint Père et à lui obéir, et presque tous sont disposés à lui obéir de grand cœur comme au chef Suprême de l'Eglise, à l'arbitre souverain dans toutes les affaires religieuses. Ils ont cependant vu des Papes se succéder et en des termes en apparence irrévocables abolir pratiquement le l'adroado, condamner et même excommunier des prêtres goanais révoltés, et puis sans un mot d'explication laisser ces documents pontificaux devenir lettre morte uniquement parce que le Portugal y faisait opposition. Le résultat est que les catholiques de l'Inde sont hors d'état d'attacher aucune importance aux documents émanés de Rome pour condamner les abus du Patronage portugais. Les mauvais catholiques savent qu'ils n'ont qu'à les combattre ou même ·faire semblant de les ignorer pendant un temps suffisamment long, et qu'ils obtiendront ce qu'ils désirent. Les bons catholiques doivent conserver une attitude passive, dans leur impuissance à venir en aide au Saint Siége. Ils sont désorientés et découragés, et ne peuvent que s'étonner de voir que le Pape cède tant d'autorité sur l'Eglise aur Indes à S. M. le Roi de Portugal.

22. Nous prions respectueusement Votre Excellence de considérer combien de fois, depuis cinquante ans, des Brefs et des Décrets ont été publiés dans l'Inde, tous également énergiques et décisifs dans les termes, et cela pour rester lettre morte ou être bientôt suivis d'autres documents contredisant les précédentes et annulant les décisions antérieures. Combien de fois les catholiques de l'Inde n'ont-

(Ex. gr. le Mémoire des chrétiens Paravors, et celui de l'East Indian Association de Bombay.) ils pas vu les représentations unanimes de leurs évêques et leurs propres pétitions regardées comme non avenues, au lieu que la plus grande déférence était accordée aux désirs d'un gouvernement étranger, faible mais intrigant, et aux clameurs d'une faction bruyante et méprisable ?

23. Nous ne voulons pas fatiguer Votre Excellence par les nombreux exemples qui pourraient appuyer ces observations. L'histoire de l'Eglise dans l'Inde pendant les cinquante dernières années, n'est que trop féconde en exemples qui prouvent les effets désastreux des concessions en faveur du Padroado. Que pouvait-il y avoir de plus clair et de plus décisif que le Bref, "Multa præclare" (28 avril 1838), qui supprimait les quatre évêchés portugais de Cochin, Crangauore, Méliapour et Malacca et limitait la juridiction de l'Archévêque de Goa aux possessions Portugaises ? Ou encore le Bref "Probe nostis" (9 mai 1853) qui ·condamnait le schisme indo-portugais et excommuniait quatre prêtres révoltés ? Pour aboutir au Concordat sans effet de 1857! Le Bref "Studio et Vigilantia" (26 août 1884) était précis et décisif. Le Saint Père y déclarait que l'Eglise aux Indes se trouvait dans un état alarmant; des troubles sérieux avaient éclaté. Il y avait lieu de craindre, disait Sa Sainteté, que la foi des catholiques ne fût en

péril, que les conversions des infidèles ne fussent arrêtées et le progrès de la religion entravé. Le Saint Père attribuait ces maux a "la double juridiction" et en conséquence il *abolissait cette double juridiction dans sept Vicariats.* Quel en fut le résultat? Le Bref resta lettre morte, et au profond découragement des bons catholiques, aux applaudissements des Padroadistes, il fut suivi du Concordat de 1886, qui consacrait pour ainsi dire et perpétuait la double juridiction.

24. A Madras l'Union Catholique vient de se former, à peu près sur le même plan que l'Union Catholique de Bombay. Ce sera le devoir du Conseil de cette Union, de mettre sous les yeux de Votre Excellence, en temps opportun, les effets désastreux que le Concordat de 1886 et la pression exercée sur le Saint Siège par le Portugal ont eus pour la paix et la prospérité de l'Eglise dans cette Présidence. Par le Concordat de 1886 Madras est devenue après Bombay le second boulevard du Padroado dans l'Inde Anglaise. En conséquence on nous a instamment prié d'informer Votre Excellence, que les catholiques britanniques de Madras et tous ceux de cet Archidiocèse, ont été vivement peinés de la façon dont leur eminent Archevêque, le Docteur Colgan, a été humilié en face de toute la population par les clauses du Concordat de 1886 en faveur d'un gouvernement étranger, tel que celui de Portugal. Ils ont été surtout sensibles à ce fait que le Portugal n'a pas permis que le Concordat de 1886 reçut sa pleine exécution à Madras.

25. Le 29 janvier 1887, Monseigneur Agliardi, l'auguste prédécesseur de Votre Excellence, mit ce Concordat à exécution dans la ville de Madras, et les catholiques qui étaient auparavant sous la juridiction goannaise, acceptèrent très volontiers d'être gouvernés désormais par Monseigneur Colgan. Deux mois plus tard l'œuvre était détruite par un ordre venu de Rome, et par déférence pour le Portugal, la double juridiction rétablie. Cette mesure rétrograde fut d'autant plus pénible au clergé et aux fidèles de l'Archidiocèse de Madras, que leur Archevêque avait dû déjà, aux termes du Concordat, sacrifier une portion considérable de son territoire au diocèse de Méliapour récemment rétabli. De plus, les schismatiques de Kottayam, de Trichur et de tout le Malabar ne peuvent comprendre les changements, que le St. Siège apporte aux decisions qu'il a declarées définitives. Ils regardent ces changements comme des preuves nouvelles contre la sagesse et l'infaillibilité du St. Siège. C'est un nouvel obstacle aux conversions : les évêques perdent la confiance des peuples, puisque la première autorité de Rome semble se contredire.

26. Nous n'avons pas la mission, et ce n'est pas ici le lieu, d'exposer tout au long à Votre Excellence les griefs particuliers des catholiques de Madras. Nous ferons seulement observer qu'à Madras comme

à Bombay les vœux et les intérêts des catholique britanniques sont entièrement méconnus. On n'a pas prêté la moindre attention aux représentations de Monseigneur Colgan, le seul prélat d'origine anglaise, excepté un, qui soit actuellement aux Indes, tandis que les concessions sont prodiguées aux sujets du Patronage portugais et aux partisans de l' *Anglo-Lusitano*. Un autre prélat anglais, Monseigneur Porter, (qui n'est plus, malheureusement), fut écouté un instant à Rome. Il réussit à mettre quelque ordre dans le chaos de la " double-juridiction" à Bombay. Maintenant qu'il est mort, ayant sacrifié sa vie pour l' Eglise de Dieu, son œuvre est ruinée par la puissante pression que l'ambassadeur du Portugal n'a pas manqué d'exercer à Rome. Pour nous servir des termes insultants de l' *Anglo-Lusitano* au milieu de son triomphe, " la Propagande a jeté un os à ronger à Cerbère."

27. Nous avons déjà parlé longuement de ce journal de Goa. Nous voulons seulement rappeler à Votre Excellence la façon dont l'*Anglo-Lusitano* traita le Décret du 17 Septembre 1887, qui, d'après celui du 25 Septembre 1888, était absolu et définitif. Ces Décrets relatifs à la double juridiction, furent non seulement traités avec insulte et mépris par l' *Anglo-Lusitano*, mais encore regardés comme non avenus par les évêques de Damaun et de Méliapour. Ces évêques n'ont jamais publié dans leurs Diocèses le Décret Pontifical de 1888. Le langage de l'*Anglo-Lusitano* était pourtant trop violent pour passer inaperçu à Rome. Dans une lettre fameuse du 21 Décembre 1888, condamnant cette feuille, le Cardinal Secrétaire d'Etat qualifia d'*insensée* la résistance des Goanais à ces Décrets. Mais que s'en est il suivi ? L'*Anglo-Lusitano* ne s'est pas soumis, et comme nous l'avons dit, l'évêque de Damaun a refusé jusqu'ici de publier la censure du Cardinal Secrétaire d'Etat. Tous les Catholiques fidèles ont attendu que le Saint Siège vengeât son autorité outragée, et prît la défense de ses évêques et de ses missionnaires si grossièrement insultés par la faction portugaise. De plus nous avons entendu dire que le 9 janvier 1889, les archévêques et évêques missionnaires de l'Inde, ayant à leur tête Monseigneur Porter, envoyèrent au Saint Siège un mémoire, dans lequel ils le prièrent de ne pas modifier son Décret, ni de céder à l'agitation goanaise précédemment condamnée. Le Saint Siège n' a rien fait de la sorte. Au contraire, toutes les concessions que l'*Anglo-Lusitano* réclamait à grands cris ont été faites. Le triomphe de l'agitation des Padroadistes, c'est à dire de ces gens que son Eminence le Cardinal Rampolla avait flétris comme "ignorants et corrompus ", est maintenant complet.

28. Nous avons dit assez pour prouver à Votre Excellence que les catholiques britanniques ont raison de dire que la politique du Saint Siège vis à vis du

Padroado dans l' Inde a eu des effets désastreux et que les catholiques fidèles sont par là confondus et profondément découragés. Nous espérons en même temps que Votre Excellence ne considérera point ces franches observations comme un acte irrespectueux. Nous nous sommes expliqués sans détour dans l'intérêt des catholiques britanniques de Bombay et de Madras parceque nous étions convaincus que Votre Excellence aimerait mieux savoir la pure vérité sur l'état de l' Eglise dans ces contrées, de personnes qui y résident, et connaître les sentiments des catholiques, tant européens qu' indigènes, qui sont soumis au pouvoir dominant dans l'Inde. Nous n'avons d'autre dessein que d' exposer le cas tel qu' il doit apparaître à la majorité des catholiques de l' Inde. De plus, c'est un fait bien connu qu'avant le Concordat de 1886, les évêques missionnaires du Sud de l'Inde, exprimèrent l'opinion unanime que, de nos jours, le Padroado était un mal sans aucun mélange de bien, et que la meilleure solution aux difficultés actuelles se trouve dans son abolition. Ils furent confirmés dans ce sentiment par le Bref "Studio et Vigilantia" donné en 1884, et l'histoire du Padroado depuis le Concordat de 1886 ne fournit aucune raison de croire cette opinion erronée.

Mémoire des Evêques de la Présidence de Madras au Secrétaire d' Etat pour l' Inde, 15 Août 1883.

29. Nous avons écrit à Votre Excellence dans toute la sincerité de notre cœur et avec une entière confiance dans votre justice et dans votre amour de la vérité. Nous pouvons vous assurer que notre seul but, à Bombay et à Madras, est de faire connaître à Votre Excellence les vrais sentiments des catholiques de l'Inde britannique, afin que les remèdes convenables puissent être appliqués à leurs maux, et que la paix et la prospérité soient rendues à l'Eglise. L'Inde est peut-être le plus magnifique champ ouvert à l'activité des missionnaires dans le monde entier, et celui qui leur promet le plus de succès. Mais à cause de l'influence néfaste du Patronage portugais, et de l'ingérence du gouvernement portugais, le travail bienfaisant des missionnaires dévoués de l'Eglise est paralysé et leur action reste stérile sur une vaste étendue de la peninsule indienne.

30. C'est un devoir bien pénible de dévoiler ainsi, même en part, les effets désastreux du 'Patronage Royal' du Portugal aux Indes. Cependant notre peine ne sera pas perdue si nous pouvons conduire tous les hommes raisonnables à la seule conclusion qui parait être inévitable,—c'est à dire, que le seul remède pour tous ces maux est d'abolir entièrement le 'Padroado' dans l'Inde britannique. Un gouvernement égoïste dans l'Europe, et une bande d'agitateurs aux Indes ont, tous les deux, abusé trop long de la faveur et de la condescendance du Saint Père. Il n'y a plus lieu pour les concessions. *Salus animarum suprema lex.* Pour que le succès de la religion Catholique devienne, un jour, possible dans l'Inde il faut détruire le ' Padroado ' de haut en bas.

Nous n'hesitons pas d'amener la question à cette conclusion-ci, qui est la seule qui soit logique. Les faits de l'histoire, et beaucoup de documents sérieux nous font savoir que, même au 17ème siècle, des Papes en succession, avaient trouvé que le Patronage portugais, établi dans l'Orient sous des autres conditions, était devenu un obstacle à la religion au lieu d'un secours, une malediction au lieu d'un bonheur.

31. Nous avons la confiance que Votre Excellence aura la bonté de faire connaître notre situation à Notre Saint Père le Pape. L'Union Catholique de Bombay ne se compose pas seulement de catholiques européens. Ses membres sont en grande majorité des catholiques eurasiens ou indigènes, tous sujets britanniques. De plus notre Union, si nouvellement établie, a déjà deux branches dans la Présidence de Bombay, l'une à Poona, et l'autre à Karwar. La dernière est composée entièrement de catholiques indigènes (chrétiens l'aravers). Nous sommes aussi autorisés à parler au nom de l'Association des ' East-Indians ' de Bombay (Bombay East-Indian Association), qui représente une nombreuse et florissante communauté de catholiques à Bombay et dans le voisinage de cette ville. Les membres sont tous sujets britanniques et ont pleinement le droit d'être écoutés, puisqu'ils sont les catholiques originaires du pays et fixés dans la contrée. Ce sont de fidèles sujets du gouvernement britannique et ils sont très sensibles aux prétendus droits de la couronne de Portugal dans l'Inde anglaise. Enfin, nous plaidons la cause des milliers de soldats irlandais qui font partie des troupes britanniques dans l'Inde, et qui n'ont nullement besoin d'un Patron portugais qui s'interpose contre eux et leur Saint Père le Pape.

32. Pour conclusion nous prions Votre Excellence respectueusement d'avoir la bonté de faire connaître nos sentiments à notre Saint Père, en l'assurant de notre amour et de notre plus profonde vénération ; afin que par là Sa Sainteté soit tenue au courant des événements, et soit bien informée des vœux et des espérances de ses fidèles enfants les catholiques de l'Inde britannique.

Afin que les autorités ecclésiastiques a Rome puissent, dans le plus bref délai possible, être informés de l'état des affaires dans l'Inde, nous avons l'honneur d'envoyer a Votre Excellence en même temps que cette lettre, sa traduction-ci en français.

Dans l'espoir de recevoir une réponse favorable.

Agréez, Excellence, l'assurance des sentiments les plus respectueux de vos très humbles serviteurs en Jesus Christ,

Secrétaires associés de l'Union
Catholique de Bombay.

Appendix I.

THE LAST DECREE ON THE DOUBLE JURISDICTION.

April 1890.

No. 1840.

Ootacomundi die 19 *Aprilis* 1890.

AMPLISSIME DOMINE.

(1.) Heic adjunctum mitto Amplitudini Tuae Illmae ac Revmae Decretum quo exercitium duplicis jurisdictionis in Indiis Orientalibus definitiva ratione ordinatur.

(2.) Ad haec meum est Amplitudini Tuae significare Sanctitatis Suae voluntatem omnimodam esse, quod ordinationes priorum Decretorum super hac materia, una simul cum modificationibus in novissimo hoc Decreto contentis nulla nova interposita mora executioni committantur.

(3.) Quae cum ita sint, non dubito quin Amplitudo Tua omnia et singula praedicta Decreta sit incunctanter in omnibus executioni adamussim commissura.

(4.) Porro rem admodum gratum mihi faciet Amplitudo Tua, si hasce literas meas illico in acceptas referre velit, pro qua humanitate Tibi in antecessum intimo corde gratias·ago .

(5.) Interim vero Deum optimum Maximum, bonorum omnium Datorem, enixe adprecor ut Tibi universisque fidelibus pastoralibus Tuis curis concreditis, omnia fausta ac felicia largiatur, et ea qua par est reverentia et observantia me profiteor

Amplitudini Tuae Illmae ac Revmae

addictissimum in Christo,

✠ ANDREAM, Archiepiscopum Acridan.

Delegatum Apostolicum in Indiis Orientalibus.

Illmo ac Revmo Domino

Domino THEODORO DALHOFF,

Administratori Aplico Archidioecesis Bombayensis.

No. 1839.

DECRETUM.

Utentes Auctoritate Apostolica, qua benignitate Sanctissimi Domini Nostri Leonis Divina Providentia Papae XIII sumus suffulti, omnibus et singulis praesentes literas inspecturis declaramus ac decernimus, quod, vi Novissimae Conventionis inter Sanctam Sedem et Regem Fidelissimum Lusitaniae de exercitio Regii patronatus in Indiis Orientalibus definitiva ratione ordinando initae, Resolutiones et Declarationes, quae continentur in respectivis decretis a Sacra Congregatione de Propaganda Fide et a Sacra Congregatione Negotiis Ecclesiasticis extraordinariis praeposita conjunctim editis mensibus Septembri et Decembri anni millesimi octingentesimi octuagesimi septimi super dubiis de exercitio duplicis jurisdictionis propositis a R. P. D. Archiepiscopo Bombayensi et a R. P. D. Archiepiscopo Goano, quaeque a Nobis per Decretum diei XIII Octobris anni millesimi octingentisimi octuagesimi octavi ad ceteras omnes Indiarum Orientalium Dioecesses in quibus duplex jurisdictio existit extensae fuere ; nec non aliae Resolutiones, quae ab iisdem Sacris Congregationibus ad earundem Resolutionum et Declarationum sive confirmationem sive explicationem datae fuerunt per aliud Decretum diei XXII Septembris ejusdem anni pariter coniunctim editum, quaeque a Nobis Archiepiscopis et Episcopis omnibus et singulis in quorum Dioecesibus duplex jurisdictio exstat transmissae fuerunt per literas diei XXIII Octobris ejusdem anni, modificantur juxta dispositiones quae inferius sequuntur.

I.

"Ordinarius Dioecesanus *pro tempore* Damaonensis munietur extraordi-
" nariis Apostolicis facultatibus, vi quarum ipse suam Ecclesiasticam jurisdictionem
" extendere poterit etiam ad omnes illos subditos Patronatus, goanae vel Lusit-
" a nae originis, qui ex quacumque Indiarum plaga in territorium Bombayense se
" conferant ut ibi resideant."

"Hanc autem gratiam concedens Sanctitas Sua intendit quod, usquedum
" communi consensu inter Sanctitatem Suam et Gubernium Lusitanum provisum
" non sit, uti Suum desiderium est, modo Sacrorum Canonum disposi-
" tionibus conformiori, hujusmodi abnormi rerum conditioni, immo ipsi bono
" respectivarum Dioecesium, nec immutari sensibiliter debeant quoad populum
" adventitium proportiones quae ad praesens existunt inter christianitates utrius-
" que jurisdictionis Bombayensis nempe et Damaonensis, nec turbari liceat
" tranquillitas et bona harmonia, quae inter respectivos Praelatos regnare debet.
" Ad hunc finem Sanctitas Sua vult quod, quam citius id fieri poterit, communi
" consensu utriusque Ordinarii, Bombayensis nempe et Damaonensis, conficiatur
" catalogus personarum, quae tempore subscriptionis Concordati anni millesimi
" octingentesimi octuagesimi sexti intra limites Archidioecesis Bombayensis
" jurisdictioni Patronatus subjiciebantur."

"Convenit autem inter Paciscentes quod hujusmodi exceptionalis concessio
" favore Damaonensis Dioecesis facta ob peculiares considerationes et praeter juris
" canonici ordinationes extendi non possit ad alias Patronatus Dioeceses.

a 2

II.

" Ordinarii *pro tempore* Dioecesium Patronatui ex Concordatu pertine.
" tium pergent exercere suam jurisdictionem in proprios subditos, etiam in casu
" quod hi ex una in aliam transeant parochiam, quae vel intra limites territorii
" continui respectivarum Dioecesium vel in Missionibus iisdem Dioecesibus aggre-
" gatis existat. Ast, hoc excepto casu fideles subditi Patronatus subjicientur
" jurisdictioni ordinariae locali, quamdiu ibi commorentur.

III.

" Quoties adfuerit necessitas aedificandi novas Ecclesias, Capellas, Scholas
" aut alia Instituta extra territoria exempta et in medio christianitatum in quas
" Episcopi Patronatus jurisdictionem tantum personalem exercent, Sanctissimus
" Pater declarat Se paratum ad excipiendas preces quae hac super re Sibi fuerint
" oblatae, et ad judicandum utrum, habita ratione incrementi fidelis populi inter
" christianitates Patronatui subjectas,adsit casus derogandi juri communi per extra-
" ordinarium privilegium. Quo quidem in casu Episcopi Patronatus extendere
" poterunt suam territorialem jurisdictionem ad haec quoque aedificia, sed prae-
" ter hunc casum peculiaris Apostolici privilegii quodcumque aedificium erectum
" extra territoria exempta, scilicet extra Ecclesias et hortos adjacentes (vulgo
" compounds) subjectum manebit jurisdictioni ordinariae locali.

IV.

" Jurisdictio disciplinaris et criminalis Episcoporum Patronatus extende-
" tur etiam ad ipsorum subditos, qui partes sunt Christianitatum suis Dioecesi-
" bus aggregatarum. Hujusmodi tamen jurisdictio non erit exclusiva ; integrum
" enim servari debet jus ordinariorum localium corrigendi et puniendi delinquen-
" tes in proprio territorio ad normam legum canonicarum."

Itaque hac tantum ratione et quoad hasce tantum partes modificantur
supradictae Resolutiones et Declarationes Sacrarum Congregationum, firmis in
omnibus manentibus ceteris respectivorum D: cretorum partibus, quae ab hisce
modificationibus non afficiuntur ; ita ut in futurum duplicis jurisdictionis exercitium
in Archidioecesibus Bombayensi, Goana, Madraspatana et Calcuttensi atque in
Dioecesibus Damaonensi, Poonensi, Meliaporensi, Daccaensi, Coccinensi et Quilo-
nensi, illis eorundem Decretorum partibus quae firmae manent atque insimul
novissimis hisce dispositionibus conformari omnino et adamussim debeat.

a 3

Omnes igitur Christifideles et presbyteri ex nunc in posterum tenentur et obligantur ex obedientia S. Sedi debita et sub poenis a jure statutis ut hujusmodi jurisdictionis ecclesiasticae determinationes servent.

Contrariis quibuscumque minime obstantibus.

Ex aedibus Delegationis Apostolicae.

Ootacamundi die XVIII Aprilis MDCCCXC.

✠ ANDREAS, Archiepiscopus Acridanus,
Delegatus Apostolicus in Indiis Orientalibus.

Ootacamund, 19th April, 1889.

No. 1840.

Very Reverend Sir,

I send herewith to your Reverence the Decree, by which the exercise of the double jurisdiction in the East Indies is definitely settled.

It is my duty to inform Your Reverence, that it is the absolute will of His Holiness, that the ordinances of the former Decrees in regard to this matter, together with the modifications contained in this last Decree should be at once put into execution.

Therefore, I doubt not, that Your Reverence will put each and all of the aforesaid Decrees in their entirety into prompt and exact execution.

Further you will do me a great favour by informing me at once, that you have received my letter for which I tender you in anticipation my heartfelt thanks.

In the meantime I pray fervently to God Almighty, the giver of all good gifts that he may shower his choicest blessings upon you and all the faithful, entrusted to your pastoral care.

Believe me,

Your Reverence's most affectionate in Christ,

✠ ANDREW, *Archbishop of Acrida.*

Delegate Apostolic in the East Indies.

To

The Very Reverend

THEODORE DALHOFF, S. J.

Administrator Apostolic of the Archdiocese of Bombay.

No. 1839.

DECREE.

In virtue of the Apostolic authority, with which We are graciously empowered by Our Most Holy Father Lord Leo XIII, by Divine Providence Pope, to all and each who may see these letters We declare and we decree, that

a 4

in virtue of the last agreement entered into by the Holy See and his Most Faithful Majesty, the King of Portugal, concerning the definite regulation of the exercise of the Royal Patronage in the East Indies, the Resolutions and Declarations, which are contained in the respective Decrees passed jointly by the Sacred Congregation de Propaganda Fide and the Sacred Congregation for the Despatch of Extraordinary Ecclesiastical Affairs in the months of September and December 1887 about questions concerning the exercise of the double jurisdiction proposed by the Most Rev. Archbishop of Bombay and the Most Rev. Archbishop of Goa, and which (Decrees and Declarations) have been extended by Our Decree of the 13th October 1888 to all the other Dioceses in the East Indies in which the double jurisdiction exists ; as well as all the other Resolutions, which were given by the same Sacred Congregations either in confirmation or explanation of the same Resolutions and declarations by another joint Decree passed on the 22nd September of the same year and which were forwarded to each and all Archbishops and Bishops, in whose Dioceses the double jurisdiction exists by Our letters of the 23rd October of the same year, are modified as follows.

I.

Let the Diocesan of Damao for the time being have Extraordinary Apostolic faculties, by virtue of which he may extend his Ecclesiastical jurisdiction also to all those subjects of the Patronage, of Goan or Portuguese origin, who come from whatever part of India into the Bombay territory, in order to reside there.

But his Holiness granting this favour wishes, that as long as no provision has been made by common consent between his Holiness and the Portuguese Government, as is His desire in a manner more in conformity with the rules of the Sacred Canons, for such an abnormal state of things, as well as for the well being itself of the respective Dioceses, the proportions which exist at present between the Christian communities of both Jurisdictions., viz., of Bombay and Damao may not be notably changed in regard to the incoming population, and that the peace and the good understanding which ought to exist between the respective prelates be not disturbed. Therefore, His Holiness wills that as soon as possible the catalogue of persons who were subject to the Patronage within the limits of the Archdiocese of Bombay at the time of the signing of the Concordat in the year 1886 be made by mutual consent of both the ordinaries, viz., of Bombay and Damao.

But the contracting parties agree, that such an exceptional concession made in favour of the Diocese of Damao for special considerations and over and

a 5

above the ordinances of Canon law can not be extended to other dioceses of the Patronage.

II.

The Ordinaries *pro tempore* of the dioceses, belonging to the Patronage according to the concordat, continue to exercise their jurisdiction over their own subjects, also in case, when those go from one parish into another, which may exist either within the limits of the continuous territory of the respective Dioceses or in missions belonging to the same dioceses. But this case excepted the faithful, subject to the Patronage, are subject to the ordinary local jurisdiction.

III.

As often as there is a necessity to build new Churches, Chapels, Schools or other Institutions beyond exempted territories and in the midst of Christian Communities in which bishops of the Patronage exercise a merely personal jurisdiction, the Holy Father declares himself ready to receive petitions, which for this purpose may be sent to him and to decide, whether, taking into consideration the increase of the faithful within the Christian communities subject to the Patronage there be a case to deviate from the common law by an extraordinary privilege. In such a case then the bishops of the Patronage may extend their territorial jurisdiction to these buildings as well, but excepting this case of special Apostolic privilege whatever building erected beyond the exempted territories, viz., churches and adjacent gardens (vulgo compounds) remains subject to the ordinary local jurisdiction.

IV.

The disciplinary and criminal jurisdiction of the bishops of the Patronage extends also to such of their subjects as form a part of the Christian communities belonging to their dioceses. However, such jurisdiction is not exclusive; for the right of the local ordinaries to call to order and to punish delinquents in their own territory according to Canon law must remain intact.

Therefore in this way only and as regards these points the abovementioned Resolutions and Declarations of the Sacred Congregations are modified, whilst the other points of the decrees, which are not affected by this modifications, remain firm in every respect, so that in future the exercise of the double jurisdiction in the Archdioceses of Bombay, Goa, Madras, Calcutta and in the Dioceses of Damao, Poona, Meliapur, Dacca, Cochin and Quilon must be altogether in exact conformity with those points of the same decrees, which remained unaltered and also with those last regulations.

a 6

Therefore all the faithful, the laity and the clergy henceforward are in duty bound in obedience due to the Holy See and under penalties laid down by law, to adhere to these resolutions concerning the ecclesiastical jurisdiction.

Any thing to the contrary notwithstanding.

Given at the Apostolic Delegation.

Ootacamund, 18th April, 1890.

(Sd.) ✠ ANDREW, Archbishop of Acrida,

Apostolic Delegate in the East Indies.

THE BRIEF 'MULTA PRAECLARE' (1838) WITH AN ENGLISH TRANSLATION.

Multa praeclare Romani Pontifices Praedecessores Nostri, pro Apostolici muneris debito, constituerunt, ut in vastissimis Orientalium Indiarum regionibus, catholicae religionis incremento prospicerent. Cum enim ob summam earum regionum ab Apostolica Sede distantiam, ob itinerum longitudinem, locorumque difficultates, ardua valde esset tantae illius vineae Domini partis cultura, sollicitudinem suam impense Romani Pontifices demonstraverunt, ut quidquid, pro diversa temporum ratione, religioni utile apud illas gentes futurum esse videretur, auctoritate sua sancirent, et studiose servandum esse juberent.

Omittimus illum curam commemorare ab Apostolica Sede nunquam neglectam, ut undique sacerdotes excitarentur ad sacri ministerii officia in iis regionibus obeunda : nihil de singulari dicimus adhibita a Praedecessoribus Nostris facilitate, ac benignitate ut, ad non retardandos iis in locis religionis catholicae progressus, innumera ferme concesserint, quibus passi sunt, cum iis gentibus remissius agi, quam ut canonum et disciplinae severioris instituta requirebant. Eam tantum hic memorabimus grati animi significationem, quam pro dignitate sua, Romani Pontifices erga illos ostenderunt, quos constabat, opera sua religioni utiles, per ea loca fuisse.

Perspicuum hujus rei testimonium continet patronatus privilegium Fidelissimis Lusitaniae Regibus ab Apostolica Sede tributum, ut diœcesium nonnullarum in iis regionibus Episcopi, eorum nominatione eligerentur. Cum enim illorum Principum pietas, ac munificentia multum contulisset, ut in vastissimis illis regionibus, Episcopatus nonnulli constitui possent, Praedecessores Nostri, grati animi testificatione eorum merita prosequi cupientes, largiti sunt, ut earum dioecesium Episcopos Sedes Apostolica eligeret, quos idoneos illi nominassent. Hujus praeterea privilegii concessione, Apostolica Sedes prospexit, ut non diuturna esset sedium illarum Episcopalium vacatio, facilius Episcopos ea loca opportunos haberent, et praesulibus ipsis satis congrua praesto essent subsidia, quae eorumdem dignitati convenirent. Factum est vero temporum vicissitudine, ut hoc, quod diu religioni utile in iis regionibus fuit, in eo statu manere non potuerit, quem Praedecessorum nostrorum decreta, in adjunctis rerum longe diversis edita, servandum esse jusserant.

Pluries Nos, cum adhuc Consilio Christiano Nomini Propagando praeessemus, perpendere rationum gravitatem debuimus, quae demonstrabant, regiones illas tam late patentes, quae permagnam vastissimae cis Gangem peninsulae partem constituunt, necessario requirere, ut Apostolica Sedes religioni in iis periclitanti succurreret, et ecclesiastici regiminis formam ea ratione moderaretur, quae obtinendae religionis incolumitati par esse posset. Notum Nobis erat, regiones illas dioecesium Cranganorensis, Coccinensis, et Meliaporensis, seu S. Thomae limitibus comprehendi. Constabat vero Nobis, Praedecessores Nostros Fidelissimis Lusitaniae Regibus patronatum in illas Dioeceses, et Episcopos nominandi privilegium impertitos esse. Hoc enim continetur literis apostolicis fel. rec. Pauli IV diei 4. Februarii anno 1557, quae incipiunt *Pro excellenti*, quibus dioecesim Coccinensem constituit; item Clementis VIII. diei 4. Augusti 1600 incipientibus *In supremo*, et Pauli V. diei 6. Februari 1816, incipientibus *Alias postquam* de Cranganorensis Archiepiscopatus erectione; ac denique, Apostolico decreto Pauli V., diei 9. Januarii 1606. quo Episcopatus Meliaporensis, seu S. Thomae constitutus est. Non omisimus vel ab eo tempore, ad bonum religionis promovendum illa omnia conari, quae temporum adjuncta patiebantur.

Postquam vero ad D. Petri cathedram, licet immerentes, evecti fuimus, multo frequentius, et omni gravitate praestantibus monumentis excitati sumus, ut religioni in permagno discrimine apud illas gentes versanti opem afferremus. Haec animo volventes, et Apostolicae sollicitudinis officia cogitantes, adducti idcirco sumus, ut literis apostolicis diei 18. Aprilis 1834. incipientibus *Latissimi terrarum tractus*, Vicarium Apostolicum a Sede Apostolica tantum dependentem constitueremus, qui populosam Calcuttae urbem, ejusque politicam praefecturam subjectam haberet. Quoniam vero reperti sunt, qui Vicarii Apostolici a Nobis instituti jurisdictioni resisterent, et Apostolicis nostris literis non obtemperandum esse contenderent, eo quod in illis, expressa mentione facta, derogatum non esset iis, quae Paulus V. die 9 Januarii 1606. de Episcopi Meliaporensis, seu S. Thomae jurisdictionis finibus decreverat, Nos, alio Brevi Apostolico, diei 4 Augusti 1835. cujus initium est *Commissi Nobis*, omnem hunc dissidii praetextum rejecimus, et plura declaravimus, quae ad stabilius firmandam Vicarii Apostolici Bengalensis auctoritatem poterant pertinere. Eadem de causa factum est, ut alium Vicarium Apostolicum Madraspatani, literis diei 25. Aprilis 1834 incipientibus *Ex debito Pastoralis*, instituendum esse duxerimus. Haec quoque ratio fuit, cur, die 23 Decembris 1836. aliud Breve Apostolicum incipiens, *Ex munere pastoralis*, ediderimus, quo vastissimam insulam Ceylon Vicario Apostolico a Nobis instituto gubernandam commisimus. Hac denique ratione factum est, ut prospicere cupientes religionis necessitati apud illas gentes, quae peninsulae partem incolunt, quae ad Orientem montium Gates vergit, et a flumine Chovery ad promontorium usque Comorinum protenditur, universum illum re

b 2

gionum tractum, qui regna Maduræ, Tanjorii, Moravae, et Misorii comprehendit, per nostram Congregationem de Propaganda fide, dis 3. Junii 1837 Ven. Fratris Clementis Episcopi Drusiparensis, in Ora Coromandelica Vicarii Apostolici, provisoria ratione, et quoad aliter a S. Sede decretum fuerit, curae et jurisdictioni commiserimus.

Intelligimus per haec, quae hactenus a Nobis de ea Indiarum regione statuta sunt, in permagna peninsulae parte religionis utilitati consultum esse. Sed praeter illa loca, quae Vicariis Apostolicis gubernanda tradita fuerunt, non parvae adhuc supersunt ibi regiones, quarum bono spirituali prospicere tenemur, quaeque inter fines dioecesium Cranganorensis, Coccinensis, et Meliaporensis, vel S. Thomae positae sunt. Scimus, disciplinam ecclesiasticam, populi mores, fidem catholicam, iis in locis, quae jamdiu pastore carent, magnum detrimentum accepisse, notumque Nobis est, praetextu defendendi, ac conservandi jura dioecesium illarum, plures abuti, ut Vicariis Apostolicis, quos Sedes Apostolica constituit, resistant, eorum auctoritatem oppugnent, et schisma perniciosum excitare conentur. Plane sentimus, Nos, ex officio, quod Deus Nobis in D. Petri successione commisit, omnino teneri, ut Ecclesiae curam in dissita etiam qualibet orbis parte geramus, eaque decernamus, quae ad religionem ubique juvandam conducere posse videmus.

Communicato igitur consilio de tam gravi re cum VV. FF. NN. S. R. E. Cardinalibus negotiis Propagandae Fidei praepositis, eorumdem sententia probata, ac matura totius negotii consideratione a Nobis instituta, Apostolicae potestatis plenitudine, haec decernenda esse judicavimus.

Videlicet, provisoria ratione, et quoad Sedes Apostolica nihil aliud novi statuerit, decernimus, regiones eas omnes, quae dioecesis Meliaporensis, seu S. Thomae limitibus continentur, quaeque hactenus nulli Vicario Apostolico commissae sunt, Vicariatui Apostolico Madraspatano uniendas esse, et jurisdictionem, atque auctoritatem totam ecclesiasticam, et spiritualem in eas regiones, ad Ven Fr. Danielem Episcopum Salditanum, Vicarium Apostolicum Madraspatani, ejusque successores pertinere. De regionibus vero, quae limitibus dioece_ sis Cranganorensis, et Coccinensis continentur, et quae nulli Vicario Apostolico hactenus traditae sunt, eadem ratione jubemus, illas Vicariatui Apostolico in Malabarica regione instituto, cujus sedes in oppido Verapoli est, uniri debere, et jurisdictionem, atque auctoritatem totam ecclesiasticam, ac spiritualem in eas regiones, ad Ven. Fr. Franciscum Xaverium Episcopum Amathensem, Vicarium Apostolicum Verapoli commorantem, ejusque successores spectare. Atque ut Malacensis quoque regio trans Gangem, Apostolicae Nostrae sollicitudinis fructus accipiat, et Religionis incolumitati, atque incremento in ea regione consulamus, universam regionem illam Ven. Fr. Friderici Cao Episcopi Zamensis, Vicarii Apostolici Avani et Peguensis jurisdictioni, eadem provisoria ratione subjicimus.

Declaramus, in earum regionum ecclesiastico, ac spirituali regimine, Vicarios Apostolicos memoratos, a Nobis, et ab Apostolica tantum Sede immediate dependere, eos solos tamquam veros regionum illarum ordinarios ab omnibus habendos esse, eisque omnes obtemperare debere, et ab illis ecclesiasticam jurisdictionem, ac facultates accipere. Derogamus propterea literis Apostolicis superius recensitis Praedecessorum nostrorum de dioecesium Cranganorensis, Coccinensis, et Melaporensis, seu S. Thomae erectione atque limitibus, it emque illis a Paulo IV. editis die 4. Februarii 1557, incipientibus *Pro excellenti*, de Episcopatus Malacensis erectione, et praeterea derogamus etiam literis Apostolicis fel. rec. Praedecessoris Nostri Pauli IV. die 4. Februarii 1557, incipientibus *Etsi Sancta*, de Archiepiscopatus Goani erectione, ita, ut nullam jurisdictionem, quocumquetitulo, etiam speciali mentione digno, in regionibus, de quibus agitur, Archiepiscopus Goanus in posterum possit exercere.

His ista ratione statutis, videmur omnino Nobis, religionis opportuno regimini per eas regiones prospexisse, ac certo speramus futurum, ut, Deo Optimo Maximo consilium a nobis initum benedicente, haec ad Ecclesiae incrementum magnopere conferant, confidimus etiam fore, ut decretis Nostris omnes ea obtemperent observantia, quae dignitati Nostrae debetur, cui in D. Petro, pascendi, regendi, ac gubernandi universalem Ecclesiam a Deo potestas tradita est. Non dubitamus denique, eos, qui hactenus voluntati Nostrae restiterunt, suscepturos esse saniora consilia, et a gravissimo schismatis malo, alienos ex animo esse futuros.

Praeter illud enim catholici cujuslibet proprium officium, ut D. Petro per os nostrum loquenti obtemperare teneatur, persuasum habemus, eos intellexisse, quae ad dissidii sui defensionem attulerunt, ipsorum repugnantiam excusare nulla ratione posse. Omnibus enim cognitum est, Apostolicam Sedem in patro͏̄ natu illo Fidelissimis Lusitaniae Regibus concedendo nunquam voluisse, impedimentum sibi ipsi inducere, quominus religioni in regionibus illis provideret, et non posset ea statuere, quae pro temporum necessitate, populi christiani salus fuisset postulatura.

Putamus, eos quoque videre, quantopere diversis temporibus, et a praesenti rerum statu distinctis, privilegium illud concessum, servatumque fuerit; existimamus illos etiam sentire, regiones eas, ad quarum bonum procurandum mentem Nostram convertimus, non amplius veteri politico regimini subesse, quo

b 4

Lusitanis Regibus facile erat in iis regionibus patronatum exercere, sed illas in potentissimi Regis ditionem devenisse, cujus gubernii forma, atque instituta, hoc minime passura esse, nobis exploratum est.

Recordamur tandem, Romanos Pontifices Praedecessores Nostros, non obstante patronatus concessione, ex diocesibus eo privilegio comprehensis, provincias separandas aliquando, et Vicariatus Apostolicos provincias illas complectentes, constituendos esse pro religionis utilitate, jure decrevisse : quare confidimus, ˙eos, qui dissidere hactenus non dubitarunt, facile perspecturos, cavendum sibi esse, ne decretis Nostris in praesenti rerum conditione latis, patronatus praetexto repugnantes, aperte ostendant, se dissidii sui nullam, nisi inobedientis animi rationem afferre posse. Decernentes has praesentes literas firmas, validas, et efficaces existere, et fore, suosque plenarios, et integros effectus sortiri, et obtinere, ac iis, ad quos spectat, et spectabit, hoc, futurisque temporibus plenissimo suffragari. Contrariis non obstantibus quibuscumque. Datum Romae, apud S. Petrum, sub annulo Piscatoris, die XXIV. Aprilis, MDCCCXXXVIII. Pontificatus Nostri anno octavo.

E. CARD. De GREGORIO.

TRANSLATION OF THE ABOVE.

THE APOSTOLIC LETTERS OF HIS HOLINESS POPE GREGORY XVI. CONCERNING THE INSTITUTION OF VICARS APOSTOLIC IN THE EAST INDIES.

GREGORY XVI. POPE.

For Perpetual Memory Hereof.

The Roman Pontiffs, our Predecessors, in accordance with the obligations of the Pastoral Office, have determined many things very expressly, that, in the most extensive regions of the East Indies, they might provide for the increase of the Catholic Religion. For whereas, on account of the very great distance of those countries from the Apostolic See, on account of the length of journeys, and the difficulties of places, the cultivation of that extensive portion of the vineyard of the Lord would be very arduous, the Roman Pontiffs have earnestly demonstrated their solicitude, to sanction by their authority, and order to be accurately observed, whatever, according to the different changes of the times, might seem likely to be useful to religion among those nations.

We omit to make mention of the care never neglected by the Apostolic See, that priests should be encouraged everywhere to perform the duties of the Sacred Ministry in those places. We say nothing of the singular favour and benignity exhibited by Our Predecessors, that, in order not to retard the progress of the Catholic Religion in those places, they made almost innumerable concessions, by which they suffered those nations to be treated more gently, than the institutes of the canons, and of a more severe discipline required. We will only mention herein that indication of gratitude, which, in accordance with their dignity, the Roman Pontiffs shewed to those, who, it appeared, were useful to religion throughout those places.

The privilege of patronage, granted by the Apostolic See to the most Faithful Kings of Portugal, that the Bishops of some Dioceses in those regions might be elected upon their nomination, contains an evident proof of this matter. For, whereas the piety and munificence of those Princes had contributed much to the founding of some Bishoprics in those most extensive regions, Our Prede- cessors, desiring to reward their merits by a testimony of their gratitude, have granted, that the Apostolic See would choose, as Bishops of those Dioceses, the persons, whom, being worthy, they had nominated. Moreover, by the concession of this privilege, the Apostolic See expected, that the vacancy of those Episcopal Sees would not be of long duration, that those places would have suitable Bishops more easily, and that due assistance would be at hand for the Bishops themselves, which would accord with their dignity. But it has come to pass, from the vicissi- tude of the times, that this, which was for a long time a benefit to religion in those countries, could not remain in that state, which the Decrees of Our Prede- cessors, published under circumstances entirely different, had commanded to be observed.

Often times, whilst as yet We presided over the Council for propagating the Christian Name, We felt it to be Our duty to weigh the importance of the reasons, which demonstrated, that those countries so widely extending, which constitute a very great part of the vast peninsula on this side of the Ganges, necessarily require, that the Apostolic See should succour religion in danger therein, and should modify the form of Ecclesiastical Government in such manner, as would be consistent with the safety of religion. It was known to Us, that those regions are comprehended within the limits of the Dioceses of Cranganore, Cochin, and Meliapore or St. Thomé. It was also manifest to Us, that our Pre- decessors had granted to the Most Faithful Kings of Portugal, patronage with respect to those Dioceses, and the privilege of nominating the Bishops. For this is contained in the Apostolic Letters of Paul 4th, of happy memory, of the 4th day of February in the year 1557, which begins, *Pro excellenti*, by which he founded the Diocese of Cochin ; likewise, in those of Clement 8th, of the 4th day of August 1600, beginning, *In supremo*, and Paul 5th, of the 6th day of February 1616, beginning, *Alias Postquam*, concerning the erection of the Archbishopric of Cranganore ; and finally, in the Apostolic Decree of Paul 5th, of the 9th day of January 1606, by which the Bishopric of Meliapore or St. Thomé was established. We have not omitted, even from that time, to make every endeavour for promoting the welfare of Religion, which the circumstances of the times allowed.

But since that We though unworthy, have been raised to the chair of Peter, we have been excited much more frequently, and by records of the utmost importance, to aid religion labouring under very great difficulty in those nations. Weighing those things deliberately, and bearing in mind the obligations of Apostolic solicitude, We have been therefore induced, to constitute by Apostolic Letters of the 18th day of April 1835, beginning, *Latissimi terrarum tractus*, a Vicar Apostolic depending from the Apostolic See alone, who would have subject to him, the populous city of Calcutta, and its political prefecture. Whereas, however, some persons were found to resist the jurisdiction of the Vicar Apostolic instituted by Us, and to contend, that obedience ought not to be paid to Our Apostolic Letters, because in them, by an express mention, We had not derogated those things, which Paul 5th, on the 9th day of January 1606, had decreed, concerning the boundaries of the jurisdiction of the Bishop of Meliapore or St. Thomé, We, by another Apostolic Brief, of the 4th day of August 1835, the beginning of which is *Commissi Nobis*, have rejected all this pretext of dissension, and have declared many things, which would tend to establish more firmly the authority of the Vicar Apostolic of Bengal. For the same reason it was, that we determined, that another Vicar Apostolic should be instituted at Madras, by a letter of the 25th day of April 1834, beginning, *Ex debito Pastoralis*. This was also the reason why, We published on the 23rd day of December 1836, another Apostolic Brief, beginning *Ex munere Pastoralis*, by which We committed the most extensive Island of Ceylon, to be governed by a Vicar Apostolic instituted by Us. For this reason, finally, it was, that, desiring to provide for the necessity of religion among those people, who inhabit the part of the peninsula, which lies towards the East of the Ghaut Mountains, and extends from the River Cauvery unto Cape Comorin We have committed the entire tract of country, which comprehends the kingdoms of Madura, Tanjore, Morava, and Mysore, through our Congregation de Propaganda Fide on the 3rd day of June 1837, to the care and jurisdiction of Our Venerable Brother Clement, Bishop of Drusiparo, Vicar Apostolic on the Coromandel Coast, in a provisional way, and until it may have been otherwise decreed by the Holy See.

b .

We understand by these things, which have been hitherto decreed by Us concerning this country of the Indies, that the advantage of Religion in a very large part of India has been provided for. But, besides those places, which have been given to be governed by Vicars Apostolic, several countries yet remain, for the spiritual good of which, We are bound to provide, and which are situated within the boundaries of the Dioceses of Cranganore, Cochin, and Meliapore or St. Thomé. We know that Ecclesiastical Discipline, the morals of the people, the Catholic faith in those countries, which so long want a Pastor, have suffered great injury, and We are well aware, that many use the pretext of defending and preserving the rights of those Dioceses, that they may resist the Vicars Apostolic, whom the Apostolic See has constituted, oppose their authority, and endeavour to excite a pernicious schism. We sensibly feel, that We, by reason of the office, which God has committed to Us in the succession of Peter, are wholly obliged, to have a care of the Church, even in every scattered portion of the World, and to decree all things, whatsoever We see would contribute to the support of Religion everywhere.

Therefore, having taken advice, on so important an affair, with our Venerable Brethren, the Cardinals of the Holy Roman Church, placed over the affairs of Propaganda Fide, the opinion of the same being approved of, and a mature consideration of the entire business having been instituted by Us, in the plenitude of Apostolic power, We judge it fit to decree as follows :

Videlicet, in a provisional way, and as long as the Apostolic See shall have come to no other new determination, We decree, that all those countries, which are contained within the limits of the Diocese of Meliapore or St. Thomé and which have been, up to this time, committed to no Vicar Apostolic, are to be united to the Apostolic Vicariate of Madras, and that all jurisdiction, and authority, Ecclesiastical and Spiritual, over those countries, belong to our Venerable Brother Daniel, Bishop of Salditan, and Vicar Apostolic of Madras, and to his successors. But, with respect to the countries, which are contained within the limits of the Dioceses of Cranganore and Cochin, and which, up to this time, have been delivered to no Vicar Apostolic, in the same way, We order, that they be united to the Apostolic Vicarage instituted in the country of Malabar, the seat of which is in the town of Verapoly ; and that all Jurisdiction and authority, Ecclesiastical and Spiritual, over those countries, belong to Our Venerable Brother Francis Xavier, Bishop of Amata, the Vicar Apostolic residing at Verapoly, and to his successors. And, that the country of Malacca beyond the Ganges may also receive the benefit of Our Apostolic solicitude, and that We

b 8

may provide for the safety and increase of religion therein, We in the same provisional way, subject that entire country, to the jurisdiction of Our Venerable Brother Frederic Cao, Bishop of Zama, and Vicar Apostolic of Ava and Pegu.

We declare, that in the Ecclesiastical and Spiritual government of those countries, the Vicars Apostolic above named depend immediately from Us, and from the Apostolic See alone, that they alone are to be regarded by all, as the true Ordinaries of those countries, and that all should obey them, and receive Ecclesiastical jurisdiction and faculties from them. Therefore We derogate the Apostolic letters above recited, of Our Predecessors, concerning the erection and limits of the dioceses of Cranganore, Cochin and Meliapore or St. Thomé, and likewise that published by the Paul 4th, on the 4th day of February 1557, beginning *Pro excellenti*, concerning the erection of the Bishopric of Malacca ; and moreover, We derogate also the Apostolic letter of Our Predecessor Paul 4th, of happy memory, of the 4th day of February 1557, beginning *Etsi Sancta*, concerning the erection of the Archbishopric of Goa, so that the Archbishop of Goa cannot in future exercise any jurisdiction, under any title whatsoever, even worthy of special mention, in the countries of which we speak.

These things being thus determined, we consider, that we have fully provided for the proper government of Religion throughout those places, and We confidently hope, that it will come to pass, that God Almighty blessing the design commenced by Us, those things may greatly tend to the increase of the Church. For We confide, that all will pay to Our decrees that obedience, which is due to our dignity to whom, in Peter, the power of feeding, directing, and governing the universal Church has been delivered by God. Finally we doubt not, that those who hitherto have resisted Our will, will be susceptible of more wholesome counsel, and become sincerely averse to the most grievous evil of Schism.

For besides that duty peculiar to every Catholic, by which he is bound to obey Peter speaking through Us, We are persuaded, that they have understood, that those reasons, which they have alleged, in defence of their dissension can by no means excuse their opposition. For it is well known to all, that the Apostolic See, in conceding that patronage to the Most Faithful Kings of Portugal, never intended to place an impediment to its providing for religion in those countries, nor to its having the power of decreasing those things, which in consideration of the necessity of the times, the salvation of the Christian people would hereafter demand.

We think, that they also see, how greatly different, and distinct from the present state of things, the times were, in which that privilege was granted and observed. We suppose that they even feel, that those countries, to provide for the good of which, We have turned our attention, are no longer subject to the old political Government, under which it was easy for the Kings of Portugal to exercise the patronage, but that they have come under the sway of a most powerful Sovereign, whose form of Government and Institutions, We are well aware, will not allow it.

Finally, We remember, that the Roman Pontiffs Our Predecessors, notwithstanding the concession of the patronage, have rightly decreed, that from the Dioceses comprehended under that privilege, provinces should sometimes be separated, and Apostolic Vicariates, embracing those provinces, constituted for the benefit of Religion. Wherefore, We confide, that those who have not hesitated to oppose Us hitherto, will easily perceive that they should take care, lest, refusing obedience to Our Decree made in the present state of things, they may openly show, that they can produce no reason for their dissension, but that of a disobedient spirit.

Declaring the present letters to be, and that they shall continue to be firm, valid, and efficacious, and that they are to have their full and complete effect, and to retain the same, and are to avail to their widest extent, those for whose concernment they have been issued, or whom they shall at any future time affect, notwithstanding any enactments to the contrary.

Given at Rome, at St. Peter's, under the Ring of
the Fisherman, the 24th day of April 1838,
of Our Pontificate the eighth year.

E. CARD. DE GREGORIO.

Appendix III.

The Brief 'Probe nostis' (May 1853) with an English translation.

BREVE SUMMI PONTIFICIS.

Venerabilibus Fratribus Episcopis Vicariis Apostolicis ac dilectis filiis Christi fidelibus Missionum Indiarum orientalium.

PIUS PP. IX.

Venerabiles fratres ac dilecti filii, salutem et apostolicam benedictionem.

Probe nostis, Ven. Fratres, nec vos penitus latet, dilecti Filii Nostri, quae dudum Pontifices praedecessores Nostri pro collato eis divinitus in B. Petro universi Dominici gregis pascendi, tuendique munere, et Supremi Apostolatus officio, ad collapsam, injuria temporum istis in regionibus Catholicam Fidem instaurandam, ac provomovendam, praestiterunt. Praeclara indesinentis ejusmodi vigilantiae hujusce S. Sedis monumenta exhibent eorumdem decessorum Nostrorum, ac praecipue fel. rec. Gregorii PP. XVI. Apostolicae Litterae, ac Sanctiones, queis extraordinaria licet ratione, prout rerum adjuncta postulabant, satis tamen, ac plene etiam pastorali earundem regionum curae ac regimini, nec non fidelium necessitatibus per antistites Apostolicos et Evangelicos operarios prospiciendum curavit. Nostis etiam quae et nos ipsi supra hanc Principis Apostolorum Cathedram inscrutabili divinae Providentiae consilio collocati, pro eadem qua tenebamur sollicitudine et onere egimus, ut opus persequeremur, quousque ordinariae Ecclesiarum formae, et institutioni inducendae, seu restituendae locus fieret. Dolendum tamen illud accidit, quod vix aut ne vix quidem cogitare quis poterat ex ipsis catholicis nempe non defuisse, qui speciocis sic prorsus humanisque obtentibus abrepti, salutaribus hujusmodi dispositionibus adversari et Supremae Christi Domini in terris Vicarii auctoritati obsistere, ac repugnare ausi sunt, et in suo crimine miserrime adhuc obfirmati videntur. De infando illo, Ven. Fratres, ac dilecti Filii, dissidio Nos loqui intelligitis, quod jamdiu per quosdam indignos Goaenses presbyteros inchoatum in istis regionibus, jugiter invalescit, maximo aeternae salutis fidelium detrimento, et ad foedissimum plane schisma absolvendum in dies magis magisque urgetur. Gliscenti malo autem hujusmodi occurrere vel ab initio et sine intermissione, ut scitis, et aberrantes presbyteros ac deceptam ab eis Catholicae plebis partem ad bonam revocare frugem in omni doctrina, patientia, et charitate non defuit Apostolica Sedes, qua in re decessoris Nostri Gregorii longanimitatem, ac studia impensa aemulari cupientes monitis, hortamentis, instructionibusque dissidentes memoratos pres-

c 1

byteros, eorumque sectatores a perditionis via retrahere conati sumus. Verum in vanum omnia cessisse compertum habetis, Venerabiles Fratres, ac merito invalescentia quotidie quae exinde religioni obvenerint damna experti, ac tamdiu discissum dilaniatumque Christi gregem Nobiscum flentes validioribus remediis opus esse perspicitis. Ad haec utique manum jam admovere, aegre licet, vel maxime adigimur ex iis, quae in regionibus insulae Ceylonae, Bombay et alibi forte, ab iisdem perturbatoribus, Machaonensis Antistitis adjumento, perpetrata esse non ignoratis, quaeque animi Nostri moerorem ac dolorem vehementer auxerunt. Intelleximus enim praedictum Antistitem nullo penitus accedente Apostolico, quod numquam ei dedimus, mandato, aut venia, easdem regiones Nostrorum, et Apostolicae Sedis hujus Vicariorum jurisdictioni subjectas percurrere, dissidentibus primoribus presbyteris curantibus, et compellentibus in illis Confirmationem, atque etiam S. Ordinationem adminstrare non extimuisse, despectis contemptisque sanctionibus Canonicis, et generalibus, peculiaribusque Apostolicis Constitutionibus, neque exemplo tantum, verum etiam verbo, indignaque concione fideles populos in sua deceptione firmare, et a debita legitimis pastoribus obedientia ac subjectione magis magisque avertere, et avocare non reformidasse. Tristissima haec nuntia ut primum ad Nos perlata sunt, datis ad Machaonensem Episcopum litteris, quam graviter deliquisset admonuimus, utque a similibus abstinens et conscientiae suae consuleret, et improbanda facta, scandalumque fidelibus illatum reparare satageret hortati sumus. Iterato item paulo post, allatis e Bombayna Missione relationibus, Antistitem ipsum commonendum duximus, additis iterum hortamentis, ut animae suae prospiceret, ac debitae reparationi satisfaceret neque ut severius, et juxta S. Canones in eum animadvertere Nos cogeret in Domino obsecravimus, paternis monitis Nostris eum obsecundaturum confidentes. Quamvis autem de obfirmata presbyterorum de quibus supra meminimus pervicacia, tot, ac molesta nimis argumenta praesto sint, ne tamen de eorum salute spem omnem abjiciamus, atque ut omnimode fideles populos, quoad Nos, ab eorum versutiis ac deceptione vindicemus, et ab aeternae, in quo illorum vestigiis inhaerentes versantur, perditionis discrimine avocemus, ad eos quoque impensiores adhuc nostras curas convertendas censemus. Inter alios vero antedictorum presbyterorum, qui jamdiu ad fovendum, propagandumque dissidium, et schisma perficiendum adlaboraut, quos poenis ac censuris Ecclesiasticis obnoxios esse patet nominatim adnotare peropportunum arbitramur eos, qui praecipui auctores illorum fuere, quae in Vicariatu Bombayno patrata sunt a Machaonensi Episcopo, scilicet *Marianum Antonium Suarez,* qui Vicarium Generalem Goani Praesulis in Bombayna regione se jactat; nec non presbyteros *Gabrielem de Sylva, Braz*

c 2

Fernandez et Josephum de Mello. Hosce in primis per amanter admonemus, et in Domino hortamur ut a nefaria ejusmodi agendi ratione tandem aliquando recedentes, et animae suae, et sempiternae aliorum saluti consulere ulterius haud immorentur. Quamquam vero Canonicis eos poenis, et Ecclesiae censuris obnoxios jamdiu se esse non lateat, eas tamen incurrisse, et suspensos a divinis, ac tamquam schismaticos et a catholica unitate seguntos habendos esse, nisi intra duos menses a publicatione harum Nostrarum Litterarum resipuerint declaramus, ac fidelibus populis uti tales designatos denunciatosque volumus. Alios item presbyteros probe noscimus, qui diu pariter aliis in regionibus teterrimum idem schisma fovere et implere conantur, prout in Madraspatana, Ceylona, Madurensi, aliisque Missionibus. Interea tamen eos nominatim arguere ac plectere abstinemus. Ea quippe spe nitimur fore ut hi quoque, quemadmodum et supra dicti sacerdotes, paternis Nostris hortamentis facilem pronamque aurem praebere, seque deceptasque a se plebes legitimis pastoribus, Nostris nimirum et Apostolicae Sedis Vicariis sujicere velint, ne et in hos quoque severius agere cogamur. Quamvis autem ex latis jamdiu, interatisque hujusce S. Sedis Decretis, Constitutionibus ac jussionibus quoad legitimos Indiarum Orientalium Pastores nullus omnino supersit ambigendi ac dubitandi locus, ad quodvis tamen effugium penitus amovendum expresse iterum et quatenus opus sit, declaramus, omnem auctoritatem ac jurisdictionem in constitutis Apostolicis Vicariatibus, Nostris et S. Sedis Vicariis, aut administratoribus competere, ac tributam, ita esse, ut nemini prorsus liceat sacra iis in regionibus munia obire, ac sacramenta ministrare, nisi de illorum venia ac facultate. Nil vero inanius quam quod ad captivandam fidelium simplicitatem jactitare feruntur hi presbyteri, permulta esse quae statuta sunt non ab Apostolica Sede, et a R. Pontifice, verum eo inscio et inconsulto a S. C. de Propaganda Fide sancita, nonnulla quoque haud attendenda, eo quod civilis auctoritatis placitum defuerit. Sciant itaque omnia ac singula ea de re statuta, a Romanis Pontificibus motu proprio, certa scientia, ac deliberatione et de potestatis plenitudine edita fuisse, et si, quae per S. Nostram Congreg. rec. mem. Decessores Nostri, ac Nos quoque decrevimus, ea quoque nedum Romanis Pontificibus Nobisque haud insciis vel inconsultis, verum etiam volentibus ac jubentibus decreta et constituta fuisse sciant ; S. quippe Congregationem Nostram nonnisi Apostolicae Sedis per Consilium adjutricem, et Mandatorum, ac Jussionum ejusdem S. Sedis ministram esse, norunt omnes. Putidum vero impiumque commentum illud est, Apostolicae Sedi divinitus collata Jura, ac traditam a Christo Domino Supremi regiminis in Ecclesia clavum potestatem humanis placitis, nutibusque arctari, praescribi aut imminui posse Incassum

c 3

Catholica Communione gloriatur qui Petri Cathedrae ac Romano Pontifici haud jungitur, quippe qui cum Eo non est contra Eum, et extra unitatem se esse fateatur oportet; quique nobiscum non colligit, dispergit. Eos autem Petri Cathedrae ac Romano Pontifici junctos agnoscere haud unquam possumus, qui Nostris ac S. Sedis Vicariis ab Eadem gubernandis fidelibus istis constitutis adversantur, ac parere detrectant. Nec praetereundum praenotatos presbyteros nedum legitimae Ecclesiae potestati, ac divinae propterea ordinationi resistere, verum etiam per ejusmodi dissidia adlaborare, ne initae inter Nos et Carissimam in Christo Filiam Nostram Mariam Portugalliae et Algarbiorum Reginam Fidelissimam, ejusque Gubernium tractationes ad optatum exitum perducantur; atque ita adversantur votis ipsius Reginae, dum ei obsequium praestare autumant. Demum et vos, dilecti Nostri filii, Christifideles alloquimur, et amantissime admonemus ac hortamur, ut eos, qui a praepositis vobis pastoribus, et a Nostra propterea Communione abstrahere adnituntur, studiose devitetis, neque ab ea, extra quam nulla salus esse potest, unitate avelli unquam patiamini. Cavete ab iis qui veniunt ad vos in vestimentis ovium, intrinsecus autem sunt lupi rapaces. Iterum vobis nuntiamus nullam prorsus Goanensibus aliisque presbyteris, qui vos conturbant, jurisdictionem et auctoritatem, aut ministerii exercendi in regionibus istis, in quibus Vicarii Nostri, et Apostolicae Sedis instituti fuerunt, facultatem inesse, ita ut nonnisi in perniciem animarum vestrarum, quousque a legitimis iisdem Praesulibus abscissi ii maneant, illis adhaereretis. Caterum in Eo fidentes qui Auctor est pacis, et Deus totius consolationis, Nobis pollicemur futurum, ut vulgatis hisce Nostris litteris inter vos, errantes in justiciae ac salutis viam remeasse, et unum ubivis ovile factum percipiamus. Interim Vobis, Ven. Fratres, et dilectis curae vestrae comissis gregibus istis Apostolicam Benedictionem peramanter impertimur.

Datum Romae apud S. Petrum, die IX. Maii anno MDCCCLIII. Pontificatus Nostri anno Septimo.

PIUS PP. IX.

c 4

TO THE VENERABLE BRETHREN, THE BISHOPS VICARS APOSTOLIC, AND TO THE BELOVED SONS THE FAITHFUL IN CHRIST OF THE EAST INDIA MISSIONS.

PIUS P. P. IX.

Venerable Brethren and Beloved Sons Health and Apostolic Benediction.

You are all well aware, Venerable Brethren, and it cannot be unknown to you Our Beloved Sons, what the Pontiff's Our Predecessors conformably to the duty divinely imposed upon them in Blessed Peter of feeding and protecting the whole flock of the Lord, and in virtue of the office of the Supreme Apostolate have heretofore done in order to reform and promote in these countries the Catholic Faith, which through the injury of times had so much suffered. Striking proofs of such unceasing vigilance of this Holy See are furnished by the Apostolic Briefs, and Decrees of our Predecessors, more particularly by those of Pope Gregory XVI., of happy memory, by which he, though in an extraordinary manner conformably to exegencies, but nevertheless sufficiently and fully caused the Pastoral care and government of these countries, as also the wants of the faithful to be provided for, by means of the Bishops Vicars Apostolic and Evangelical Labourers. You know also what We Ourselves, by the unsearchable counsel of Divine Providence placed on this Chair of the Prince of the Apostles, have done by reason of the same solicitude and burden, as in duty bound, that we might pursue the work until room be made for introducing or restoring the ordinary form and institution of Churches.

Nevertheless it unfortunately happened, what seemed impossible to suppose viz., that even amongst Catholics there were not wanting some, who, completely carried away by specious and human pretexts, dared to oppose such salutary arrangements and resist and impugn the authority of the Supreme Vicar of Jesus Christ on earth, and who are seen still to continue most miserably obstinate in their crime.

You perceive, Venerable Brethren, and Beloved Sons, that we speak of that abominable dissension, which stirred up some time back by certain worthless Goanese Priests in these countries, is gradually increasing to the greatest detriment of the eternal salvation of the faithful, and which is daily more and more pushed on, in order to effectuate the foulest Schism; but the Apostolic See did not fail, as you are aware, to resist the growth of such an evil from the very beginning and without intermission, and in all Doctrine patience and charity to bring back to their duty the erring Priests, and that portion of the

c 5

Catholic people deceived by them. In which matter, being desirous to imitate the forbearance and earnest study of our predecessor Gregory We endeavoured to withdraw by admonitions, exhortations, and instructions the said dissenting Priests and their followers from the way of perdition.

But, Venerable Brethren, you see indeed that all has proved useless, and after having experienced the daily growing injurious hereby inflicted upon Religion and deploring with us, Christ's flock so long rent asunder and torn into pieces you fully understand, that more energetic remedies become necessary. We therefore feel, that We must now apply our hand to this work and We are though reluctantly, compelled thereto, more particularly by the deeds recently effected by these Agitators, with the assistance of the Bishop of Macao, in the territories of the Island of Ceylon, Bombay and perhaps in other parts, of which you are not ignorant, and which have exceedingly increased the sorrow and pain of Our heart. For We learnt that the aforesaid Prelate, without being furnished with either any Apostolic Mandate which We never gave him, or permission passed through those countries subject to the jurisdiction of our Vicars and of this Apostolic See where yielding to the prayers and urgent entreaties of the chiefs amongst the dissenting Priests, he was not afraid to administer Confirmation, and even Holy Orders in spite and contempt of the Canonical decrees and general as well as particular Apostolic constitutions, and that he not only by example, but also by word, and unworthy preaching did not dread to confirm the faithful people in their deception, and to alienate and summon them away more and more from the due obedience and subjection to their legitimate Pastors.

No sooner had these most afflicting news reached Us than We sent letters to the Bishop of Macao, wherein we pointed out the grievous wrong he had done and admonished him to refrain from similar acts, to consult his conscience, and to be careful in repairing the scandal given to the faithful. Shortly afterwards the reports from the Bombay Mission having reached Us, we thought proper again to warn that Prelate once more with fresh exhortations, that he should look to his soul and should make due reparation, and trusting that he would comply with Our paternal admonitions, We entreated him in the Lord not to compel Us to proceed more severely, nor to enforce against him the sacred Canons.

Notwithstanding the existence of the many and but too painful proofs of the determined obstinacy of the Priests of whom We made mention above, nevertheless in order that We may not give up all hope of their salvation, as also that by all means We may deliver the faithful people, as far as we are able, from their craft and deceit, and rescue them from the danger of eternal perdition in which they are whilst following their footsteps, We think it proper, We should direct towards them also Our particular care. Now among others of the afore said Priests, who for length of time labour in fomenting and propagating dissension, and in establishing the Schism, who it is clear are liable to ecclesiastical penalties and censures, We think it very proper to notice by name those, who were the principal Authors of what has been perpetrated by the Bishop of Macao in the Vicariate of Bombay viz. Mariano Antonio Soares, who boasts himself to be the Vicar-General of the Goa Prelate in the Bombay territory, as also the Priests Gabriel DeSilva, Braz Fernandes, and Joseph DeMello.

These in particular We admonish and We most affectionately exhort them in the Lord, to cease now at least from such impious doings, and to delay no longer to look after their own souls, and the eternal salvation of others. But although they are not ignorant, that they are liable to canonical penalties and ecclesiastical censures, nevertheless We declare, unless they return within two months from the publication of this Our Brief, they shall be held to have incurred them, to be suspended *a divinis*, and to be *Schismatics*, and separated from the *Catholic unity*, and We will that they be branded and denounced as such by the faithful people.

We are also fully aware, that there are other priests, who have long endeavoured to foment and effect in other countries the most heinous Schism, such as in Madras, Ceylon, and other Missions, We however for the present refrain from reproving and punishing them by name; for we entertain the hope, that they, as well as the above mentioned priests will give an easy and willing ear to Our paternal exhortations, and that they will submit themselves and the people deluded by them to their legitimate Pastors, viz., Our Vicars and those of the Apostolic See, in order that We may not be compelled to proceed more severely against them also.

Now though in virtue of long since enacted and repeated Decrees and constitutions and commands of this Holy See, as regards the legitimate Pastors of the East Indies, there does not remain the smallest room for wavering or doubting; nevertheless in order to remove all subterfuge, We declare again positively, and as far as it may be necessary, that in the established Apostolic Vicariates, all authority and jurisdiction belongs, and is committed to our Vicars or Administrators, and those of the Holy See, in such manner, that nobody whosoever shall be allowed to exercise in the same territories sacred functions, or to administer the Sacraments, save with their leave and faculty.

But nothing is more frivolous, than what is said to be the const.

ant boast of those priests in order to beguile the simplicity of the faithful viz: that very many things are decreed, not by the Apostolic See and the Roman Pontiff, but are enacted by the Sacred Congregation *de Propaganda Fide* without his knowledge or counsel. Moreover that several matters are not to be complied with, because destitute of the *placet* of the Civil Authority; let them know therefore, that all and every of those things decreed in this matter, have been enacted by the Roman Pontiffs on their own determination, *(proprio motu)* with full knowledge and deliberation, and in the plenitude of their power, and if Our predecessors of happy memory, or even We, have decreed certain matters through Our said Congregation, let them know that they have been decreed and ordained by Our will and command, and that of the Roman Pontiffs, and not without their knowledge and counsel. For all men know, that Our Sacred Congregation is nothing more than an Assistant in counsel of the Apostolic See, and a Minister of the mandates and commands of the self same Holy See. It is indeed a foul and impious device, that the rights divinely conferred upon the Apostolic See and the power of the keys of the Supreme government on the Church delivered by Christ the Lord can be restricted, proscribed or diminished by human ordinances. In vain does he glory to be in the Catholic Communion, who is not joined to the Chair of Peter, and to the Roman Pontiff: and whosoever is not with him, must needs acknowledge to be against him, and out of Unity, for whosoever does not gather with Us, scattereth. Now we can never recognise those to be joined with the Chair of Peter, and the Roman Pontiff, who oppose and refuse to obey Our Vicars, and those of the Holy See constituted by the same See for the government of those faithful. Nor is it to be passed by in silence, that the above mentioned Priests resist not only the legitimate Church authority and consequently the Divine Ordinance, but through these their dissensions labour moreover, that the negociations already entered into, between Us, and Our most dear Daughter in Christ Maria the Most Faithful Queen of Portugal and Algarves and her Government, should not be brought to a happy issue, and so they oppose the wishes of the Queen herself, whilst they imagine to do her a service.

Lastly we address also You, Our Beloved Sons the faithful and We admonish You most affectionately, and exhort You to avoid carefully those who endeavour to withdraw you from the Pastors set over you, and therefore from Our communion, and that you will never suffer yourselves to be separated from that Unity, out of which there can be no salvation. Beware of those, who come to you in the clothing of sheep, but inwardly are ravening wolves, We again inform You that in the Goanese Priests and others who disturb you, there is no jurisdiction and authority whatsoever, nor any faculty for exercising the sacred ministry

c 8

in those territories, in which Our Vicars and those of the Apostolic See are established; so that you would only adhere to them to the ruin of your souls, as long as they themselves remain cut off from their legitimate Prelates.

For the rest trusting in Him, who is the Author of peace, and the God of all consolations We entertain the firm hope, that after this Our Briefs has been spread amongst you, the erring will return to the way of justice and salvation, and that We may everywhere behold but one sheepfold.

In the meantime We impart to You, Venerable Brethren, and to those beloved flocks committed to your care most affectionately the Apostolic Benediction.

Given at St. Peter's in Rome the ninth day of May 1853, the seventh year of Our Pontificate.

(Signed) PIUS P.P. IX.

(True translation) Fr. MAURICE,

Pro-Secretary to the Bishop of Derbe,

Administrator Apostolic of Bombay.

c 9

Appendix IV.

The Brief 'Studio et Vigilantia' (August 1884.)

LEO. P. P. XIII.

Ad futuram rei memoriam.

STUDIO ET VIGILANTIA mirabili Romani Pontifices decessores Nostri omnia semper circumspexerunt, ut in longinquis Indiarum orientalium regionibus christiana religio, jam inde ab eo tempore quo his locis offulsit faustis incrementis in dies effloresceret et fidei integritas sarta tecta servaretur. Id tum sacrae expeditiones Apostolicae Sedis auspicio jussuque susceptae, tum dioecesium et Apostolicorum Vicariatuum institutiones, tum Sacrorum Antistitum designatio, lataeque leges in eorumdem Vicariatuum procuratione servandae testantur. Sed labentibus annis vafer humani generis inimicus intercessit, et exortis deinde dissidiis inter clerum jurisdictioni Venerabilis Fratris Archiepiscopi Goani obnoxium et Apostolicos Vicarios, provisoria ratione ad ea dirimenda, visum est extraordinariam providentiae formam adhibere circa curam et administrationem eorum locorum quae extra Goanam Dioecesim sita Dioecesium Suffraganeorum terminis continebantur, quaeque tunc a Vicariorum Apostolicorum auctoritate et obedientia segregata erant. Eaque de causa eidem Archiepiscopo Goano extra ordinem et ad praefiniti temporis spatium delegata est jurisdictio in praefatis regionibus nomine S. Sedis Apostolicae exercenda, cujus praefinitum temporis intervallum pluries prolatum fuit. Jamvero ex nunciis Nobis allatis, certissimisque documentis constitit religiosam orientalium Indiarum conditionem pluribus abhinc annis minus recte se habere, adeo ut ex gravibus perturbationibus metuendum sit ne catholicorum fides periclitetur, et infidelium ad illam conversio, necnon religionis impediatur incrementum. Miseram hanc illarum regionum conditionem considerantes perspeximus praecipuam esse causam duplicem nempe, quae in iisdem locis ab utraque auctoritate libera exercetur, jurisdictionem et vastissimam illarum regionum amplitudinem, qua Archiepiscopus Goanus impar est illis advigilando pastorali, qua opus esset, sollicitudine. Quare ex officio Supremi Apostolatus divinitus Nobis demandati, sempiternaeque tot animarum salutis jactura permoti remedium tantis offerre malis cupientes, duplici huic jurisdictioni in iisdem regionibus exercendae finem imponendum esse et quae praesertim ad Vicariatus Apostolicos Hyderabadensem, Pondicheriensem, Calcuttensem, Peninsulae Malayensis, Bengalensem Orientalem, Columbensem, et Jaffnensem pertinent, componenda censuimus. Itaque mature omnibus hac de re consideratis et expensis de consilio tum Venerabilium Fratrum Nostrorum S. R. E. Cardinalium Christiano no:rini pro; agando, tum Venerabilium Fratrum Nostrorum S. R. E. Cardinalium ecclesiasticis negotiis extra ordinem expediendis praepositorum, per d cretum hujus postremae Congregationis die I. Aprilis hoc anno editum jussimus extraordinariam, quae ab Archiepiscopo Goano ex hujus Sanctae sedis delegatione exercetur in praedictis Vicariatibus Hyderabadensi, Pondichoriensi, Calcuttensi, Peninsulae Malayensis, Bengalensi Orientali, Columbensi et Jaffnensi jurisdictionem ad sex menses tantum, nempe usque ad trigesimum mensis Septembris hujusce anni MDCCCLXXXIV diem prorogari. Quo termino exacto, Archiepiscopi Goani in dictis vicariatibus jurisdictionem omnino finem habere volumus, exindeque eadem loca Vicariorum tantum Apostolicorum jurisdictioni et auctoritati integre subjici decernimus atque edicimus, et Goani Archiepiscopi jurisdictonem ex delegatione Apostolica extra ordinem eidem in iisdem regionibus impertitam a prima Octobris hujus anni die in omnibus desiisse declaramus et jubemus. Proinde universo illarum regionum clero et populo praecipimus, ut a prima praedicti mensis Octobris die dicto audientes sint iisdem Vicariis Apostolicis, iisque pareant, atque ab ipsis tantum opportunas facultates jurisdictionemque excipere debeant. Non obstantibus Constitutionibus et Sanctionibus Apostolicis, certerisque omnibus quamvis speciali atque individua mentione ac derogatione dignis in contrarium facientibus quibuscumque. Hortamur denique omnes et singulos sive e clero sint sive e populo dictarum regionum, ut uno corde et anima una suos Vicarios tamquam proprios Pastores unice cognoscant, eorumque salubria monita reverenter excipiant et impleant, ut Christiana Religio, cujus incolumitas caritate continetur, detrimentum ne capiat, et ipsi in Romani Pontificis obsequio et communione, ut par est, constanter permaneant.

Datum Romae apud S. Petrum sub Annulo Piscatoris die XXVI Augusti MDCCCLXXXIV Pontificatus Nostri Anno Septimo.

F. CARD. CHISIUS.

Translation of the Brief " Studio et vigilantia," 26th August, 1884.

LEO POPE XIII.
For perpetual Remembrance.

Ever since the Christian Religion began to illumine the distant countries of the East Indies, the Roman Pontiffs, Our Predecessors, have with admirable solicitude and vigilance, and by all means in their power, endeavoured to promote its continuous growth and prosperity, and to preserve unimpaired the integrity of the faith. The missionary expeditions undertaken under the auspices and pursuant to the commands of the Apostolic See, the creation of Dioceses and Vicariates Apostolic, the appointment of Bishops, and the enactment of laws for the right government of the

d 2

said Vicariates, bear witness to this fact. But in the course of time, the crafty foe of the human race interposed ; and dissensions having subsequently arisen between the clergy subject to the jurisdiction of our Venerable Brother the Archbishop of Goa and the Vicars Apostolic, it was deemed proper, in order to settle those differences, to provide by way of a temporary and extraordinary measure for the care and administration of such places as were situated outside the Diocese of Goa, and within the limits of the Suffragan Dioceses, yet were at that time severed from the obedience and authority of the Vicars Apostolic. With this view, an extraordinary and temporary jurisdiction over those places was delegated to the said Archbishop of Goa, to be exercised by him in the name of the Holy Apostolic See, and the limited time originally appointed for its exercise has since been frequently prorogued. However, from informations by Us received and from documents entirely trustworthy, it has become evident that the religious condition of the East Indies for several years past has been unsatisfactory ; so much so indeed, that from the grave disturbances which have taken place, there is reason to fear lest the faith of Catholics be imperilled, the conversion of infidels to that Faith impeded, and the growth of religion thwarted. Upon a close consideration of this unfortunate state of things, it has appeared to Us that its cause was to be traced chiefly to the double jurisdiction there exercised by two independent authorities, and to the impossibility in which the Archbishop of Goa was placed from the immense extent of those countries, to watch over them with due pastoral solicitude. Wherefore, pressed by the obligations of the supreme Apostleship divinely entrusted to Us, moved at the sight of so many souls that perish, and wishing to apply a remedy to evils so great, We have resolved to put an end to the exercise in those countries of that double jurisdiction, and in particular, to settle what regards the Vicariates Apostolic of Hyderabad, Pondicherry, Calcutta, the Malayan Peninsula, Eastern Bengal, Colombo and Jaffna. Having in consequence maturely considered and weighed all concerning this affair, with the advice of Our Venerable Brothers the Cardinals of the Holy Roman Church belonging to the Sacred Congregation of the Propaganda, and also of Our Venerable Brothers the Cardinals of the Holy Roman Church of the Congregation of Extraordinary Ecclesiastical Affairs, We have, by decree of the latter Congregation of the 1st April this year, ordered that the extraordinary jurisdiction which the Archbishop of Goa, in virtue of a delegation of this Holy See, exercises in the aforesaid Vicariates of Hyderabad, Pondicherry, Calcutta, the Malayan Peninsula, Eastern Bengal, Colombo and Jaffna, should be prorogued to six months only, that is, up to the thirtieth day of September of this year, 1884. It is Our will that after this term, the jurisdiction of the Archbishop of Goa in the said Vicariates do cease altogether, and We decree and enact that from that day henceforth, the said places should be entirely subjected to the jurisdiction and authority of the Vicars Apostolic; and We declare and order that the extraordinary jurisdiction imparted to the Archbishop of Goa by Apostolic delegation in the said countries, shall cease in all of them from the 1st day of October of the present year.

Therefore, We direct the whole Clergy and people in those countries to submit to the Vicars Apostolic from the 1st day of the said month of October, to obey them, and to receive from them only the necessary jurisdiction and faculties, all Apostolic Decrees and Constitutions and any thing else whatsoever, however deserving of special and individual mention and derogation, to the contrary notwithstanding.

Lastly, we exhort all, Clergy and Laity in the said countries, to acknowledge with one heart and soul their Vicars as their only Pastors, to receive and put in practice their salutary admonitions so that the Christian Religion, which is kept sound by charity may suffer no damage, and themselves may, as it is meet, persevere in their allegiance to and communion with the Roman Pontiff.

Given at St. Peter's under the Fisherman's seal on the 26th day of August, 1884, in the seventh year of our Pontificate.

F. CARD. CHIGI.

4 d

Appendix V

A LETTER FROM CARD. RAMPOLLA TO MGR. AJUTI.

Your Excellency,

I understand that a small paper entitled *O Anglo-Lusitano* is being published in Bombay, the aim of which is wholly directed to encourage a party of resistance to the ordinances issued from the Holy See.

After the perusal of some of its numbers, I am in a position and in duty bound to communicate to you the sad impression felt by me, and, at the same time, the displeasure felt by his Holiness, to whom I reported the matter. For this paper, as if it had no other object in view than to keep the torch of dissension lit up between the two ecclesiastical jurisdictions existing in India, after the last *Concordat*, does not omit any occasion to cast gross insults against the Venerable Bishops dependent upon the Propaganda and their Missionaries ; it speaks of them in the most unbecoming manner, it treats them as usurpers of others' rights, while on the contrary they enjoy the full confidence of the Supreme Pastor of the Church, and were sent to India, under his orders, to promote the good of the faithful and the conversion of the heathens, which they had carried out in the past, and are doing now amid universal admiration.

Moreover, as if invested with great and extraordinary authority, it thinks it lawful to discuss and most bitterly censure the Decrees and Acts of the Roman Congregations, feigning not to know, what is known to everybody else, that they are the medium through which the Holy See communicates its ordinances to the Catholic world.

And it cannot be otherwise than with the most malignant art, and with the intention to deceive simple people more easily, that after having passed such censures, it eulogises the wisdom and benignity of the Holy Father, Leo the XIII., humbly protesting to him its deepest subjection and obedience. For the Decrees published of late by the Holy See, through the medium of the Sacred Congregations of Propaganda, and of Extraordinary Ecclesiastical Affairs, as is proved by their tenor, were approved and confirmed by the same Supreme Pontiff. Therefore they represent the very absolute will of the Supreme Head of the Catholic Church, to whom all, without exception, the Faithful and even the Bishops, if they will correspond to their vocation, and not separate them-

e 1

selves from the Apostolic communion, must submit and obey. Consequently disobedience to such decrees that had been declared absolute and definitive, is an act of rebellion against the authority of the Supreme Pontiff, who sanctioned them.

Moreover the same paper does not spare any trouble to find adherents to this insane resistance to the Decrees of the Pontiff, which by it is considered lawful, and excites Catholics to rebellion by appealing to the passions of corrupt ignorant people. To this end it gave its effectual support in promoting a meeting, which took place at Bombay in November last which though not a respectable one, on account of the class of people that took part in it, was still very deplorable in consequence of the schismatic spirit with which the leading members were animated. For every one knows that in the Catholic Church it is not permitted to laymen to mix themselves in discussions regarding religious matters and to raise protests, even in the shape of petitions, against acts emanating from the Holy See and by it declared definitive after long and careful deliberation. To pretend to instruct the Bishops and the Supreme Pontiff himself in what they should do for the good of souls and to preserve justice ; to say that the Supreme Pontiff was not well informed when he prescribed certain rules of conduct to the faithful ; to declare that the acts of the Supreme Pontiff, determining the exercise of the ecclesiastical jurisdiction were issued without the knowledge of places and circumstances of time, and in violation of the rights of others, or that they are not binding on the consciences of the faithful, is a crime of intolerable presumption, and manifests the plan of sowing schism in the Church.

Therefore to remove the scandal that such a publication might produce amongst Protestants and infidels, as though in the Catholic Church there might exist dissensions, that are opposed to the necessary subordination of the faithful to the hierarchical power, I wish that the Ordinaries would declare that this paper *O Anglo-Lusitano* is extremely to be reproved, and that it is reproved by the Holy See, and that it does not represent, in the least, the ideas and principles which can in any way be tolerated by Catholicism or which may be reconciled with the sentiments of the true Catholic profession.

In order that no one should be deceived by the semblance of zeal and respect towards the Supreme Pontiff, with which, abusing the simplicity and good faith of many, the *Anglo-Lusitano* carries on its work of sowing dissensions between the children of the same Church, it would be very opportune that the

e 2

Bishops, in the way that they shall think most efficacious, should put the faithful on their guard, by inculcating on them their duty of obedience to the Holy See.

Your Excellency will use this my Despatch to treat on this weighty subject with every one of the Bishops in whose Diocese this paper is circulated.

I take this occasion to renew the sentiment of my profound esteem.

Your Excellency's
Most affectionate in Christ,
M. CARDINAL RAMPOLLA.

Rome, 21st December, 1888,
MGR. ANDREA AJUTI,
Delegate Apostolic in the East Indies.

PASTORAL LETTER OF HIS GRACE THE ARCHBISHOP OF BOMBAY.

GEORGE

By the Grace of God and favour of the Apostolic See Archbishop of Bombay.

to

Our Reverend Brethren the Clergy, Secular and Regular, and our Beloved Children, the Faithful Laity of the Archdiocese.

HEALTH AND BENEDICTION IN THE LORD !

For good reasons, beloved children in Christ, We have hitherto observed silence. We rejoice that the letter of His Eminence allows Us to speak openly to you and to condemn in the strongest terms this mischievous paper, the *Anglo-Lusitano.* We recommend you not to subscribe to it, not to read it ; we put you on your guard against it ; receive its statements very cautiously ; mistrust its history, and its theology, reject its Canon Law utterly ; in one word, look upon the paper as an unsafe guide on all religious questions. Lastly, We warn all connected with it, those who provide the funds which carry it on, those who write in it, and those who take any part in the printing or management, that they are accomplices in a sinful work.

The objects for which it exists are to oppose the Holy See, to upset the decrees of the Holy Father and his Congregations, to encourage feelings of hatred, to prolong dissensions and to lead away from the Church simple, uneducated people. To attain these objects it employs insulting language against

e 3

priests and Bishops, against the Delegate of the Holy See in India, and against the Holy Father himself, aggravating its attacks on the chief pastor of the Church by hypocritical professions of loyalty and respect.

The *Anglo-Lusitano* further assumes the office of critic and adviser to all the authorities of the Church from the Holy Father down to the Vicar. It sits in judgment " with intolerable presumption" on their conduct and administration : it advises, almost dictates, how they are to discharge their sacred duties, how they are to arrange the course of studies in their seminaries, how they are to preach, in one word, how they are to do the work of a Bishop or a priest.

You are aware that the civil law in India allows great liberty, it might be called license, to the Press in the discussion of political and social questions : not a few of the native papers abuse this liberty and give much offence to right-minded persons, who are sincere friends of India. The *Anglo-Lusitano* carries into the discussion of Church matters the license which is a disgrace to secular papers writing on secular subjects.

You, beloved children in Jesus Christ, naturally ask yourselves, who has given such authority to the *Anglo-Lusitano* ? What are the qualifications of its writers ? If the civil authority leaves them free, how about the ecclesiastical authority ? What sanction and support have they received from the Church ? Cardinal Rampolla has told you they have received none : they write in defiance of the Church. They may be named and paid by a committee ; they may have assumed the work themselves ; in any case they are mere laymen, who have no commission from the Church.

If the writers were all men of standing, men of intelligence, men well-informed, men versed in theology, and Church history and Canon Law, men conspicuous for their piety and edifying lives ; if they were even priests, holy and learned priests, they could not without " intolerable presumption" pronounce judgment on Bishops and on the Holy See.

Cardinal Rampolla's letter to the Apostolic Delegate bears the date of December 21st. A few days previously, on December 17th, the Holy Father addressed a letter to the Archbishop of Tours who had censured an excellent Catholic journalist for having in his paper found fault with the nomination of a certain priest to a Bishopric. The Pope approved the step taken by the Archbishop. His Holiness says amongst other things :—

" Certainly it is intolerable that laymen, professing to be Catholics, should take upon themselves to denounce and to criticise, in the columns of a

o 4

paper, without any restraint, according to their own good pleasure all manner of persons, not excepting Bishops, and to think that everyone is free to hold what opinions he likes, except on matters which are of divine faith and to act as he pleases.

" In the case before Us, Venerable Brother, you have every reason to count on Our support and approbation. Our duty obliges Us to watch and to labour that the divine authority of Bishops be preserved intact and sacred. It is Our duty, too, to order and insist that it be everywhere held in honour and that none of the obedience or honour due to it be withheld by Catholics.

" For the Church, that divine edifice rests in very deed, as on a foundation visible to all, first upon Peter and his successors, and then upon the Apostles and their successors, the Bishops. To hearken to them or to despise them, is to hearken to our Lord Jesus Christ Himself, or to despise Him. The Bishops form by far the most venerable portion of the Church, that portion which by divine right teaches and rules men : and for this reason whoever resists them or obstinately refuses to obey their word, separates himself from the Church. (Matth. 18,17.) Nor is obedience to be confined to matters bearing on faith ; it must be carried much further, to all matters that come under Episcopal authority.   *   *   *   *   *   *

" It is ·indeed certain and clear that there are in the Church two orders quite distinct, the shepherds and the flock, the leaders and the people.

" The duty of the first is to teach, to govern, to guide men through life and to lay down rules for them : the duty of the other is to live in subjection to the first, to obey, to observe its rules, to show it reverence. If those who ought to be subjects usurp the place of superiors, they not only act rashly and disorderly ; as far as in them lies, they upset the order of things so wisely appointed by God. Should there chance to be found in the ranks of the Episcopacy a Bishop not sufficiently mindful of his dignity, who seems unfaithful to some of his duties, he does not on that account forfeit any of his authority ; as long as he remains in communion with the Roman Pontiff no one under his jurisdiction has any right t o refuse him reverence and obedience.

" On the other hand private individuals are not justified if they inquire into and criticise the acts of Bishops ; this is reserved to those who wield a superior authority in the hierarchy, above all to the Supreme Pontiff: for to him Jesus Christ has committed the charge of feeding all the sheep as well as all the lambs. At the outside, when serious cause for complaint exists, it is lawful to refer the matter to the Roman Pontiff, yet quietly and prudently, as zeal for the public welfare requires, not with loud outcries and violent statements, which tend rather to create division and hatred or to increase them."

With these weighty words from the Chair of St. Peter We conclude, once more warning you against this mischievous paper the *Anglo-Lusitano* and its un-Catholic principles ; once more reminding you that it has been reproved and condemned by the Holy See, and exhorting you to pray the Holy Ghost to change the hearts of its promoters that they may repent and hereafter consecrate to the service of the Church and the maintenance of charity the time and the labour they have mis-spent in opposing her and her sacred ministers.

We direct that this Our Pastoral Letter be read and explained tc the people by all Parish Priests and Chaplains at the chief Mass on the first Sunday after they receive it.

Given at Our residence, Fort Chapel, Bombay, on the Feast of the Desponsation of Our Lady, January 23rd, 1889.

✠ GEORGE,

Archbishop of Bombay.

PASTORAL OF HIS GRACE THE ARCHBISHOP OF MADRAS.

To the Clergy and Faithful of the Archdiocese of Madras.

DEARLY BELOVED IN CHRIST.

The accompanying letter, from His Eminence M. Cardinal RAMPOLLA, to His Grace the Most Rev. A. AJUTI, Delegate Apostolic in India, will, we are sure, be read with the deepest interest by all, who have the interests of our holy religion at heart, and who desire to render that obedience and reverence, which is an essential part of our duty, to whatever instructions and ordinances emanate from the Supreme Head of Christ's Church on earth. It will also fill us with a holy indignation to find, that amongst those, who claim to be called Catholics, there should be found some, who whilst they eulogise the wisdom and benignity of the Holy Father, and who under the garb of sheep's clothing, are still found to be ravening wolves, seeking to foment discord amongst the faithful, and encourage resistance to the ordinances issued by the Holy See. It is our unhappy lot to have in our midst, here in India, some so-called Catholics, we trust they are but few, who, animated by a most unholy and most malignant spirit, would attempt to deceive innocent people and lead them to believe that

e 6

resistance to the rules laid down for our guidance by Christ's Vicar on earth, was allowable, nay even a duty, in order to maintain their own schismatical views: a crime justly declared to be an intolerable presumption on their part. For our own part, and on the part of the Faithful of this Archdiocese, we proclaim aloud that the articles in " *O Anglo Lusitano*," will have no other effect on us, than that of making us adhere more closely to the Holy See, and proving by our obedience and perfect submission to every ordinance, that comes to us, stamped with the Seal of the Fisherman, the Seal of authority on every thing that concerns the Church of Christ on earth, that even the very semblance of schism or disobedience will not be tolerated amongst us.

We therefore warn our flock against the pernicious teaching of the "*Anglo Lusitano*," and we condemn and reprove its schismatical attempts to sow the seeds of discord amongst the children of the Catholic Church in India, and declare it to be unworthy of any support from the Faithful of this Archdiocese. That it was not condemned before by the Holy See, is owing to no other cause than the great forbearance, charity and benignity of the meek and humble Pontiff, Leo XIII, whom may our good God long preserve to rule over the Church of Christ, and guard it from all error by the wisdom of his teaching. Heartily concurring in every sentiment of His Eminence's letter, we recommend a careful perusal of it to the Catholics of the Archdiocese. It will be a consolation to them to know, that the Venerable Bishops and their Missionaries throughout India, dependent on the Propaganda, enjoy to the fullest extent the confidence of the Supreme Pastor of the Church, and that their past and present work in this portion of our Lord's vineyard are, in the opinion of His Holiness, deserving of universal admiration.

I remain,

Yours most affectionately

in Christ

✠ J. COLGAN.

Archbishop of Madras.

Catholic Cathedral, Madras, 18th January, 1889.

٢٤

Appendix VI.

DE ORE TUO TE JUDICO.

(*Catholic Watchman.*)

We have asserted, and we assert again, that the Concordat of 1886 does not represent the real wishes or original intentions of the Holy See in respect to the Church in India, and we hardly think it necessary to give proofs of a thing so evident to all, who have taken the trouble to consider the case. To believe for instance that it is better that Catholic Bishops should be chosen by a layman than by the Pope, is a doctrine which needs no serious refutation. To believe that the Pope himself thinks so, is a doctrine which deserves even less remark. To maintain that the Concordat of 1886, which tolerates the Double Jurisdiction, represents the wishes or intentions of the Pope is to falsify his own utterances as expressed only two years previously in the Brief *Studio et vigilantia.* But although it is unnecessary to develop these points, it may perhaps be opportune to shew that the Portuguese Government itself has admitted that our view is correct. We therefore reproduce some extracts from documents published by that Government in 1887 in its *Livro Branco.*

Documentos apresentados às Cortes. Negociação da Concordata de 23 de Junho 1886 sobre o Padroado da coroa Portugueza na India. Lisbon *National Press,* 1887.

But first of all we must anticipate a subterfuge common to the champions of the "Padroado." We shall perhaps be told by them that our extracts or some of them refer only to the wishes and feelings of the Sacred Congregation of Propaganda and not of the Pope himself. Our first extract will dispose of this artificial and oft-condemned distinction.

(1.) *Extract from reply of the Cardinal Secretary of State* (15th April 1885) *to a Memorandum submitted by the Portuguese Ambassador.*

"According to the expressions of the same Memorandum, "the missionaries sent by the Propaganda to the East Indies "have always violated the right of the Kings of Portugal, and "in contravention of the intentions of the Pontiffs, who sent "them, instead of founding new missions among the infidels, "in the places, in which the Portuguese were not established, "invaded their missions and churches, possessed themselves of "the rights of the ecclesiastics of the ' Padroado' and with all "craftiness usurped their Jurisdiction. With regard to this, "facts and documents relating to the last two centuries, are "cited up to the period of the conclusion of the Concordat [of "1857], and it is declared that ' the possession of many "properties and churches in which the Propagandist "missionaries find themselves is illegitimate and abusive.' "First of all, we must firmly protest against such "unjust accusations, repeated over and over again in the "Memorandum. They do not strike the missionaries alone, but "redound as a true accusation against the Sacred Congrega- "tion of the Propaganda, by whose order and under whose "direction they were sent.

" And here must be removed *the artificial distinction* between "the *Sovereign Pontiff and the Sacred Congregation,* which is "found, not only in this, but in many other Portuguese docu- "ments, produced in the long course of this unfortunate nego- "tiation. In these documents to frequent demonstrations of "humble reverence to the Chief of the Catholic Church are "opposed continual insults to the Propaganda, as if it were an "entity, which acted according to its own will and not according "to the inspiration and direction, which it receives from the "Pontiffs. Now against such imputations, Pius IX of holy "memory formerly protested in the celebrated Brief *Probe "nostis* (1853), defending the Propaganda with the following "well known words and accepting the full responsibility for its "acts :—' Every one knows that Our Sacred Congregation is " ' nothing more than an assistant in council to Us and a minis- " ' ter of Our commands and orders.' So that these accusations "cast directly at it, really strike the Holy See, which must "have allowed such invasions to take place, or have excited the "illegitimate action of the missionaries of the Propaganda. Nor "must we fail to protest very strongly against the bad treat- "ment to which these are subjected and also against the very "designation of ' Propagandist' continually applied to them in "mockery in order to make this term a sign of contradiction "and insult, as if in place of having the sublime quality of "preachers of the Gospel, sent to the Gentiles by the Supreme "Pontiff Himself, they were a gang of malefactors transported "to India, to invade the harvest of others, to destroy flour- "ishing missions and to disperse the flock of Christ. Those "who abandon the delights of the land of their birth, and all "that is dear to them, and willingly have very often to endure

"great hardships and perils to spread the kingdom of Christ "on earth, are undoubtedly very badly rewarded with such "bloody insults."

This important extract clears the ground and we now proceed to others. After worrying the Pope for many years to execute the Concordat of 1857, without making the slightest serious effort to remove the difficulties pointed out to King Louis I in Pius IX's letter of 3rd Augt. 1864, the Portuguese Government at last, frightened by the Brief *Studio,* began to negotiate for a new Concordat. It must be remembered here that the Pope, in all he has done, and in all he has proposed, has acted solely for the good of souls. The Portuguese Government, on the other hand, has never pretended to be ruled by such a motive. Now let us read the confession of the Portuguese Government expressed by the first proposition made by the Holy See in the course of the negotiations. Observe that the Holy See intended to abolish the Double Jurisdiction every where, and the proposal undoubtedly represents the wishes and intentions of the Pope and the maximum indulgence He was disposed to shew :—

(2.) *Extract from a letter, dated 20th March 1885, from the Minister of Foreign Affairs at Lisbon, to the Portuguese Ambassador at Rome.*

. . . "And what does the Holy See propose? I will repro- duce here its proposal in the same terms, in which they are "formulated in the above-mentioned note of H. E. the "(Cardinal) Secretary of State:—

"1. To the Archbishop of Goa, would be conceded the "highly honourable title of Patriarch of the East Indies.

"2. He would exercise Metropolitan rights over his Province "and preside over National Councils of all the East Indies, "with primatial rights.

"3. *In Portuguese territory* would be created two or three "dioceses, suffragan to the Archbishop of Goa, to which can be "aggregated some peoples of English territory.

"4. In the localities, where the number of faithful, subject "*de facto* to the Archbishop of Goa, is considerable, the *cura "animarum* would be confided to Portuguese or Goanese priests, "nominated by the Archbishop of Goa, on the presentation of "the local Bishops.

"5. The jurisdiction of the Archbishop of Goa, on the other "points of English territory would have to cease.

"6. Portuguese foundations and interests would be taken "into account, and settled in the way, which might seem most "conformable to equity and justice.

"Some few and succinct observations will suffice to show "that *this proposal is the complete annihilation of the rights "of the Royal Portuguese ' Padroado, which till now* [mark the "impudent falsehood !] *no Supreme Pontiff, including the pre- "sent, judged that he could or ought to derogate in any thing.*"

The Minister went on to stigmatise the proposed concessions, which the Pope judged more than sufficient to satisfy the Government, as "a flagrant violation of public faith," to threaten him with a breach of diplomatic relations, with troubles in Portugal and schisms in India. The Minister even took upon himself to calumniate the Archbishop of Goa, and to assure the Holy See, that if any measure like the Brief *Studio* was executed, that prelate would go into schism and resume the metropolitan jurisdiction, over the whole extent of the suffragan dioceses. The Minister also said his agents would be instructed to bring civil actions to get back "usurped (*sic*) churches and properties," Lest there should be any mistake, the Minister ended up by saying with great unc- tion that if the Pope did not yield, then "it will only remain "for the Government of his Majesty to follow firmly the line "of proceeding [the wicked, schismatic line !] it has traced out "and to hope that the indignation of Almighty God and of "the Blessed Apostles, St. Peter and St. Paul, which the differ- "ent Supreme Pontiffs invoke against all those who dero- "gate from the rights of the Royal Patron, without his "express consent, will formulate themselves in the public voice, "and bring the clamours for justice to the ears of the present "Vicar of Christ." In a letter dated 8th June 1885, the Cardinal Secretary of State spoke of the very painful impres- sion this abominable document had made upon the mind of the Pope, who continued, however, to maintain His original proposition.

(3) *Extract from the letter of the Portuguese Ambassador at Rome to his Government, 10th April 1885.*

"His Eminence said that he hoped the negotiations would "not encounter great embarrassments on the part of the "Government of His Majesty. I replied that *if the Holy See*

" shewed itself more reasonable in its pretensions, agreement would
" be easy."

(4.) In a letter to his Government on 16th May, 1885, the
Ambassador writes : " It is easy to see that the Propaganda
" has resolved to exercise its influence on the Catholic press
" of Germany in the sense of its pretensions...... ." or in
" other words, that the Pope has resolved to curtail the Pad-
" roado" and abolish the Double Jurisdiction. The Ambas-
" sador adds " unhappily in my opinion every thing goes and
" conspires to deprive the Crown of Portugal of its rights to
" ecclesiastical jurisdiction (sic) in British India."

(5) *Extract from letter of the Portuguese Ambassador at
Rome to his Government,* 11th June 1885

* * * " *The tenacity with which the Holy See sustains its first
" proposals* is not surprising : they are due to the exigency of
" the Propaganda."

(6) In this place we may give another extract from
Cardinal Jacobini's important Memorandum, the one from which
we took our first extract. The Portuguese Government
publishes it to its own confusion, as a convincing answer to
its objections to the first proposal of the Pope.

" We conclude then by asking the following questions :—

" " If the documents of the Holy Apostolic See, conformably to
" the known maxims of Canon Law, undoubtedly make clear
" the limits of the primitive concession of the 'Padroado,' if the
" history of the times following fully justifies the line of conduct
" hold by the Pontiffs during two centuries, if the difficulties
" which the Holy See in the year 1864 opposed to the execu-
" tion of the Concordat [of 1857] are still waiting for a reply,
" which can really satisfy it, *is it reasonable to demand new
" condescensions from the Pope?*

" If the documents of the history both ancient and modern
" of the Indian missions prove completely that the missionaries
" of the Propaganda with their own forces have created almost,
" all the present Christian community of the Indian Peninsula,
" that they have never usurped the rights of any one, but
" that they went to India, in docile obedience to the invitation
" of the Chief of the Church : that in fifty years they
" have endowed almost exclusively the new Church of Indo-
" China, of Hindustan and of Ceylon with the contributions of
" Europe, of the British Government and of the Christians them-
" selves : that they have there founded institutions and establish-
" ments of education superior to all without exception, and all
" this by their own efforts alone. If incontestable proofs
" show on the other side the reality of the disorders
" excited by the Gonnese party, the usurpations of jurisdiction,
" excesses in the use of faculties, the small fruit of their
" missions, the want of aptitude and of means to take the place

" of the present missionaries of the Propaganda. If all this
" true, can it still be maintained plausibly ' that good reason,
" natural and divine right, the public faith of treaties ask and
" ' demand that the emissaries of the Sacred Congregation
" ' should hand over to the Portuguese missionaries the houses of
" ' the Lord, and the flocks they have usurped, and go to preach
" ' the Gospel, where the name of Christ is not known ?' We
" ' leave the answer to reasonable and unprejudiced persons."

We do not think we need multiply extracts. What we have
given suffice to prove our original proposition that the Portuguese had admitted in its own publications that the Concordat
does not represent the real wishes of the Pope with respect to
the Church in India. The whole book is one long condemnation
of the Portuguese Government out of its own mouth. On the
one hand the Holy See is presented to us as moved by zeal for
the good of souls while on the other hand the Portuguese
Government presents itself as thwarting the Pope at every stage
and using threats to prevent him from carrying out his
original intentions.

On the 26th Dec. 1885, the Holy See had to make a new
proposal : that also was declined. The Ambassador wrote on
the 31st of the same month "Portugal is unable to lose any-
thing it possesses." The Pope himself appealed to the King
of Portugal on the 6th January in the following year and it was
not till April that failing to obtain better terms, the Holy See
at last consented to tolerate the miserable Double Jurisdiction
but only in Bombay and Madura. We say nothing of the other
concessions, which had to be made before the Portuguese
Government would come to terms, or of the several further
concessions, which had to be made after the Concordat was
signed, and even now we do not know how many more will be
demanded before it is fully executed.

To sum up : the Portuguese Government itself has published
the original proposals of the Pope, by which the " Padroado "
was to be curtailed to narrow limits, and the Double Jurisdiction abolished. It has shewn that by its own threats and
opposition it caused the Pope to abandon those proposals, and
ultimately to accept the present Concordat, in which the Double
Jurisdiction is maintained and the sphere of the "Padroado"
enlarged. Of our original statement that the Portuguese Government has admitted that the Concordat does not represent the real
wishes of the Pope, no further proof is necessary. Our first and
fifth extracts are of permanent importance. They will remain
as a Papal judgment, (brought to light by the Portuguese
Government itself) against the " Padroado " in these latter
times, and they ought to silence those, who continue to sneer
at " Propagandists," and expect us to shew our gratitude to
the Portuguese nation for ancient services by a humble submission to the wishes of its present Government.

Appendix VII.

EX FRUCTIBUS EORUM COGNOSCETIS EOS.

(Madras *Catholic Watchman*.)

In dealing with the question of the Double Jurisdiction, we have to contend with a certain amount of ignorance among good people and even among ecclesiastics. who, happily for themselves, have no personal knowledge of the fruits of that miserable institution. It may be thought we are fighting for a sentiment, or that we have some strange prejudice against the Portuguese nation. We are therefore compelled to publish the Judgments passed by the Holy See itself on the Double Jurisdiction, and we have to do so at the risk of causing some pain. We would prefer to be silent on the subject, but when attempts are made to misrepresent the Holy See, we have no alternative but to speak out for the instruction of our readers. On this occasion we translate a Papal document, which was published by the Portuguese Government itself in 1887. It is, we confess, a very painful one to read and reveals a state of affairs, of which Catholics cannot be proud. Some will be astonished at such a revelation, but it is no revelation to the Missionaries of the Dioceses of Pondicherry and Trichinopoly and of other places. It is just, however, to add that in Madras itself for many years we have had no grave scandals to deplore, nor here can any reflexion be cast upon the conduct of the clergy of the "Padroado." But in many isolated places the case is different, and even in some of them the Goanese clergy are the victims of circumstances, for which the responsibility falls not on them but on the Royal Patron.

Since the arrival of the Bishops of the "Padroado," there has also been, as was to be expected, a revival of discipline, but even with the best intentions on all sides, the Double Jurisdiction will never cease to be a grave calamity.

There are three important documents, which people must read, if they wish to understand the question. The first is the Memorial of the Bishops of the Madras Presidency to the Secretary of State on 15th August 1883. There the civil evils of the Double Jurisdiction were pointed out, and the Bishops concluded with the following words :—

"The condition to which the Catholic Church in India is "reduced by this Double Jurisdiction, is a source of great regret "to all who have the welfare of Christianity at heart, and who "desire to see charity and peace reign, not only amongst Chris- "tians in general, but also in Christian families. It is a perpe- "tual cause of dispute amongst priests and their flocks, more "especially on the occasion of marriages, when it is hard to "determine to what jurisdiction the parties belong, as it some- "times happens that the members of the same family belong to "different jurisdictions."

The next document is the letter we now publish, in which the Pope details the religious objections to the Double Jurisdiction, and the third is the Brief *Studio et vigilantia*, by which He tried to abolish it. Then at last the Portuguese Government woke up, and by its threats and opposition secured the Concordat of 1886, which perpetuates the Double Jurisdiction. That Government has since frustrated the efforts of the Holy See to mitigate its evils, as may be seen from the Decree which was issued on 18th April, 1890. With Cardinal Jacobini, speaking for the Pope himself, we demand the "free action of the Church" as necessary in India, and it is precisely the "Padroado" which renders that free action impossible.

Letter from H. E. Cardinal L. Jacobini, Secretary of State, to the Marquis of Thomar, Portuguese Ambassador to the Holy See.

Vatican Palace, *10th April*, 1884.

In the very beginning of his Pontificate, on the occasion of the prorogation of the extraordinary faculties of the Archbishop of Goa, demanded by the Royal Portuguese Government in 1876, our Holy Father directed his attention to the state of the Catholic Church in the East Indies, and the increasing development of those new Christianities was the object of his Apostolic solicitude. And while he found reason for joy and consolation in the flourishing condition and the progressive increase of the Churches directed by the Vicars Apostolic, which induced him to increase the number of Vicariates, he could not fail to deplore the state of decay and the grave disorders, which take place among the faithful confided to the cares of the Goanese clergy.

Extensive and authentic reports, addressed to the Holy See, from various points of the East Indies, agree in attesting in a precise and incontestable way, enormous abuses in the exercise of the sacred ministry, ignorance and religious abandonment of the people, reprehensible traffic, scandalous intrusions, violent conflicts. In many places the children are only baptized at the age of three, of four and sometimes of twelve years. Marriages are blessed in the closest degrees of consanguinity, without canonical dispensation, and without proof of the free state, and also very often the nuptials of supposed widows are authorised, while the first husband is still alive. The Sacrament of penance is only administered once a year, and without any proof of repentance, public sinners, persons notoriously living in concubinage, and men given to sorcery and necromancy are admitted to the sacraments.

In parochial churches there is only a sermon once or twice a year on the occasion of some solemnity. The religious festivals and the most celebrated sanctuaries are profaned by obscene dances, scandalous scenes and pagan superstitions authorised by the presence of the priest. The Holy Eucharist is only reserved in the churches during Lent. No care is taken of the sick, who, abandoned after confession scarcely ever receive the last sacraments and often die without the assistance of the priest, who, having all his care in receiving the fees which pertain to him, is not accustomed to be absent at the funeral or the interment.

The schools are far from corresponding to the necessities and to the extent of the parishes, and often Jews and Muhammadans of wealthy families are preferred to poor Christian boys The teaching of the catechism is completely neglected, nor do the people know the fundamental mysteries of the Faith and the obligation by which they are bound to use the sacraments : in various villages the value of the Mass above that of other public prayers is not distinguished, and in some it happens even that the name of the Divine Author of the Church is unknown.

From these facts it is easy to understand what is the culture and the conduct of the Goanese priests. Generally not possessing the most elementary theological knowledge, of an undisciplined temper and independent even of their own Archbishop, rather than promote the good of the faithful, they fix their minds on augmenting their own incomes in the exercise of the holy ministry It is not therefore surprising that without any authority and contrary to all right, they intrude themselves in administering baptism, in blessing marriages radically null for want of jurisdiction, and in burying the faithful, who belong to the obedience of the Vicars Apostolic. Similar usurpations have continued for a long time, nor are there wanting cases of injurious publications, of calumnious persecutions organised against the same Vicars, of abominable artifices to throw back into paganism villages converted by them, of violent occupation of their churches and of public tumults, as is attested by the infinite series of lawsuits and appeals, which are preserved in the records of the English Courts and of the Government of India.

In the midst of a pagan people, in the presence of schismatical oriental sects obstinately attached to their errors, it is easy to understand how such conflicts become prejudicial to the increase and to the honour of the Catholic name. The people, ill-instructed and abandoned to themselves, who, seldom visited by the priest, see him more intent on his own gain than on their spiritual good, naturally are reduced to live a pagan life, or, as happen in various villages, miserably return to paganism. The continual and bitter disagreements between two classes of ministers of the same religion, and the two-fold rule followed by them in moral judgments, and in the administration of the Sacraments, produce scandal and confusion in the minds of men, which enfeeble their faith and repel from the Church the pagans, who ought to be invited to it by the divine attractions of a religion of charity, truth and justice.

This deplorable situation was presented to the examination of a special Congregation of Cardinals in 1881, when the last prorogation of the extraordinary faculties of the Archbishop of Goa was under consideration. These most eminent Fathers were unanimous in recognising the urgent necessity for remedying such grave abuses, and in indicating to the Holy Father *as the only efficacious remedy* the abolition of the jurisdiction of the Archbishop of Goa over the *statu quo* in all the Vicariates Apostolic of the East Indies. In spite of this his Holiness, animated with sentiments of special predilection for his Most Faithful Majesty, and moved by the spirit of noble moderation, was pleased to concede the prorogation demanded for two years, and in this interval, ordered that in the same places should be newly collected more exact and certain information, and that a general and circumstantial report should be drawn up upon the religious condition of those Churches. The Sovereign order was faithfully executed, and he who writes these pages has before him the long and detailed report upon the state of the delegated jurisdiction, which confirm substantially the irregularities, which have been above enumerated, and it concludes as "follows:—"Many of these Christians live like pagans ; some "villages have relapsed entirely into heathenism; others will "soon follow, if a prompt remedy is not applied to the abandon- "ment in which the Goanese priests have left them."

The Holy See has not failed on various occasions

make known to the Portuguese Government its painful apprehensions with respect to the deplorable state of the churches of the East Indies, sometimes in conceding the repeated prorogations of the delegated jurisdiction, limiting it to three, to two years and even to one year, sometimes by means of the verbal manifestations of its representatives, and principally in the memorable letter of 3rd August 1864, addressed to his Most Faithful Majesty by his Holiness Pius IX, in which were pointed out the many obstacles by which the action of the Pontiff and of the Vicars Apostolic was impeded, the injuries done to and the persecutions raised against their holy ministry, the schismatical resistances, the repeated invasions and *other fatal consequences of the Double Jurisdiction*, and the two principal causes of these evils were demonstrated, to wit, the character of the Goanese clergy, and the enormous extent of the territory.

The disposition of the Goanese people is notorious. They consider the ecclesiastical state as a common profession or a civil career, in which they are accustomed to put their sons, in order that they may obtain means of gain and of subsistence. In this way is easily explained the want in many of them of divine vocation (which is the base of abnegation and of the ecclesiastical virtues), their deficiency in instruction, their negligence in the holy ministry, the frequent tumults and their spirit of self interest and independence. The present Archbishop of Goa —it is right to mention it—employs all his prudent zeal to maintain discipline and diminish disorders, but in regions so vast, the direction of the prelate becomes inefficacious, if it be not obeyed with reverent docility, and be not seconded by a good clergy, well-instructed and active.

It is impossible to think that such evils can be stopped by marking out the limits of the Dioceses suffragan to Goa,* for, in the first place, the four or five new dioceses would be absolutely insufficient to promote the conversion of hundreds of millions of infidels, and to satisfy the necessities of those churches, spread over a territory equal in extent to the whole of Europe which, with difficulty, are administered by twenty-five Vicars Apostolic, whose number goes on increasing year by year. Besides this, to erect new dioceses, which may be true centres of action and of religious progress, especially in the local circumstances peculiar to the East Indies, it is not enough to mark out their boundaries, like those of a property or a state, and to nominate Bishops, but Chapters, Seminaries, Schools, Religious orders, institutes of education and charity are also necessary, and above all, a virtuous, learned and zealous clergy, conscious of its high mission, and solicitous for the salvation of souls. Now to prepare all this, abundant material means are wanted, *numerous Missionary Colleges* † the unlimited and vigorous life of religious congregations,‡ in a word, the

---

* This was always the contention of the Portuguese Government that four or five paper dioceses of the "Padroado" would serve to take the place of 25 Vicariates Apostolic!

† Portugal possesses only one Missionary College, and even that is not a Missionary College in the full sense of the title.

‡ The laws against religious orders are still in force in Portugal, and in 1887 when to provide for the needs of Portuguese colonies and them alone it was proposed to modify the law, only five Members of the Portuguese Parliament, including the proposer, were in favour of the motion. The Most Faithful Nation has indeed sunk very low.

---

free action of the Church and all those conditions of which there is a splendid synthesis in the above mentioned letter of Pius IX, and which till now have not been complied with.

Nevertheless, the Holy See has not failed to give proofs of the most ample condescension, lending itself to maintain the *statu quo* in the precise terms of the agreements and settlements. It had only promised to delegate the jurisdiction over the *statu quo* for six years, and to concede a prorogation after the six years within limits more stricted. Nevertheless, twelve prorogations have already elapsed, and another of equal extension is demanded after nearly thirty years since the original concession, without any sign or guarantee presenting itself that this precarious state of things is to come to an end.

The Holy Father, having carefully weighed this important matter in all its extent, is persuaded that the religious situation of the East Indies presents most grave disorders, which expose the faith of Catholics to continual perils, and impede the conversion of the Heathen and the increase of religon. He has recognised also that the *Double Jurisdiction exercised in the same places by two autonomous authorities is the principal cause of such disorders*, and that the repeated prorogations conceded for so many long years tend to maintain and perpetuate them. Moved, therefore, by the sacred duties which His divine mission and Apostolic Ministry impose on Him, pre-occupied with the enteral salvation of so many souls, after mature deliberation He has determined, that the extraordinay jurisdiction of the Archbishop of Goa upon the *statu quo* in the twenty-five Vicariates Apostolic in the East Indies must cease ere long. Seeking, however, to give a last proof of deference for his Most Faithful Majesty and his government, he has ordered that the said jurisdiction, in conformity with the annexed decree, be prorogued for a year in the territories of Bombay, Mangalore, Madura, Verapoly, Quilon and Madras, and for six months in all the others.

And in order that this his sovereign determination may be complied with peacefully and regularly, he desires to proceed in agreement and good intelligence with the Government of his Majesty, to which will be conceded all the facilities and benevolent aid, which may be necessary to remove the obstacles to practical execution, and which are advisable on account of the delicacy of the circumstances. He has therefore ordered the undersigned Cardinal Secretary of State to invite the Government of his Majesty to take without delay those resolutions which correspond to the just needs of the crown, to the interests of its subjects and the glories of the Portuguese name without in any form compromising the flourishing state of the Vicariates Apostolic and the fututre progressive development of those Churches.

And this is what the undersigned Cardinal Secretary of State, has to communicate to his Excellency in answer to his esteemed note of the 3rd of last January, asking him to kindly bring it to the knowledge of his Government, and while he hopes the occasion opportune, in order that within the term established, the decrees may have their fulfilment, he avails himself, &c., &c.

L. CARDINAL JACOBINI.

www.ingramcontent.com/pod-product-compliance
Lightning Source LLC
Chambersburg PA
CBHW020233090426
42735CB00010B/1674